GoodFood
Dinner-party dishes

10 9 8 7 6 5 4 3 2 1

Published in 2012 by BBC Books, an imprint of Ebury Publishing.
A Random House Group Company

The Random House Group Limited
Reg. No. 954009

Addresses for companies within the Random House Group can be found at
www.randomhouse.co.uk

A CIP catalogue record for this book is available from the British Library.

The Random House Group Limited supports The Forest Stewardship Council (FSC®), the leading international
forest certification organisation. Our books carrying the FSC label are printed on FSC® certified paper.
FSC is the only forest certification scheme endorsed by the leading environmental organisations, including
Greenpeace. Our paper procurement policy can be found at www.randomhouse.co.uk/environment

To buy books by your favourite authors and register for offers visit www.randomhouse.co.uk

Printed and bound by Firmengruppe APPL, aprinta druck, Wemding, Germany

Commissioning editor: Muna Reyal
Project editor: Sarah Watling
Designer: Kathryn Gammon
Production: Lucy Harrison
Picture researcher: Gabby Harrington

ISBN: 9781849905299

MIX
Paper from
responsible sources
FSC™ C004592
www.fsc.org

Picture credits

BBC *Good Food* magazine would like to thank the following people for providing photos. While every effort has been
made to trace and acknowledge all photographers we should like to apologise should there be any errors or omissions.

Marie-Louise Avery p65, p161; Peter Cassidy p13, p27, p67, p119, p121, p123, p129, p135, p141, p157; Jean Cazals p109,
p189; Ken Field p57; Will Heap p45; Lisa Linder p203; Tim Macpherson p117; Gareth Morgans p23, p49, p71, p127, p149,
p183, p187, p201; David Munns p11, p17, p25, p31, p35, p41, p43, p75, p107, p115, p131, p143, p175, p205; Noel Murphy
p197; Myles New p33, p47, p51, p63, p79, p81, p103, p111, p133, p155, p163, p177, p191, p209; Stuart Ovenden p15, p59,
p61, p95, p113, p165, p173; Lis Parsons p29, p39, p73, p83, p87, p93, p137, p139, p145, p147, p159, p193, p195; Maja
Smend p19, p37, p99, p105, p169; Simon Smith p185, p207; Roger Stowell p53, p55, p125, p179; Debi Treloar p69, p181;
Philip Webb p21, p85, p89, p101, p151, p167, p171, p211; Simon Wheeler p77; Jon Whitaker p91, p97, p153

All the recipes in this book were created by the editorial team at *Good Food* and by regular contributors to BBC magazines.

weekend GoodFood
Dinner-party dishes

Editor **Lucy Netherton**

Contents

Introduction

The idea of a dinner party can sometimes seem a little overwhelming; whether it's deciding on the menu, the thought of spending too much time in the kitchen, or feeding guests with various food issues. However, this book will take the stress out of dinner parties and make them fun for host and guests alike.

Whatever the occasion – a romantic supper for two, birthday meal for six or feeding a crowd at an informal party – this book is packed with inspirational ideas. With everything from pre-dinner cocktails and nibbles to delicious puddings it really is a one-stop shop for your dinner party planning.

For me, the 'make-ahead' recipes are lifesavers. When entertaining guests, spending too much time in the kitchen can really spoil the mood, so having something pre-prepared in the fridge or freezer is ideal.

Whatever your skill level, there are recipes to suit everyone. The simple but special dishes look fabulous but the secret is they are all really easy to do! Take the *Prawn bruschetta with lemony fennel salad*, it takes just 20 minutes to prepare but looks and tastes spectacular!

Seasonal and special occasions are also catered for, with recipes for *Black velvet baby cakes* as the ideal ending to a St Patrick's Day dinner, or *Christmas pudding cake pops* to give out as sweet treats for friends and family over the festive season.

We know you'll have as much fun trying these recipes as we have choosing them, and I am sure you will turn to this book time and time again as you entertain through the years.

Lucy

Lucy Netherton

Notes and conversion tables

NOTES ON THE RECIPES
• Eggs are large in the UK and Australia and extra large in America unless stated otherwise.
• Wash fresh produce before preparation.
• Recipes contain nutritional analyses for 'sugar', which means the total sugar content including all natural sugars in the ingredients, unless otherwise stated.

OVEN TEMPERATURES

Gas	°C	°C Fan	°F	Oven temp.
¼	110	90	225	Very cool
½	120	100	250	Very cool
1	140	120	275	Cool or slow
2	150	130	300	Cool or slow
3	160	140	325	Warm
4	180	160	350	Moderate
5	190	170	375	Moderately hot
6	200	180	400	Fairly hot
7	220	200	425	Hot
8	230	210	450	Very hot
9	240	220	475	Very hot

APPROXIMATE WEIGHT CONVERSIONS
• All the recipes in this book list both imperial and metric measurements. Conversions are approximate and have been rounded up or down. Follow one set of measurements only; do not mix the two.
• Cup measurements, which are used by cooks in Australia and America, have not been listed here as they vary from ingredient to ingredient. Kitchen scales should be used to measure dry/solid ingredients.

Good Food is concerned about sustainable sourcing and animal welfare. Where possible humanely reared meats, sustainably caught fish (see fishonline. org for further information from the Marine Conservation Society) and free-range chickens and eggs are used when recipes are originally tested.

SPOON MEASURES

Spoon measurements are level unless otherwise specified.

- 1 teaspoon (tsp) = 5ml
- 1 tablespoon (tbsp) = 15ml
- 1 Australian tablespoon = 20ml (cooks in Australia should measure 3 teaspoons where 1 tablespoon is specified in a recipe)

APPROXIMATE LIQUID CONVERSIONS

metric	imperial	AUS	US
50ml	2fl oz	¼ cup	¼ cup
125ml	4fl oz	½ cup	½ cup
175ml	6fl oz	¾ cup	¾ cup
225ml	8fl oz	1 cup	1 cup
300ml	10fl oz/½ pint	½ pint	1¼ cups
450ml	16fl oz	2 cups	2 cups/1 pint
600ml	20fl oz/1 pint	1 pint	2½ cups
1 litre	35fl oz/1¾ pints	1¾ pints	1 quart

Crab, lime & chilli toasts

For a more relaxed dinner for two, serve these instead of a starter.

TAKES 15 MINUTES ● MAKES 8
½ small baguette, cut into 8 slices
1 tbsp olive oil
85g/3oz white crabmeat
½ red chilli, deseeded and finely
   chopped
½ tbsp chopped coriander leaves
zest and juice ½ lime

1 Heat oven to 200C/180C fan/gas 6. Put the baguette slices on to a baking sheet, drizzle over half the oil, add some seasoning, then bake for 5 minutes until golden at the edges.
2 Meanwhile, mix the crab, chilli, coriander, lime zest and juice with the remaining oil and some seasoning, then spoon on top of the toast just before you serve.

PER SERVING 71 kcals, protein 4g, carbs 7g, fat 3g, sat fat 0.4g, fibre 0.5g, sugar 0.8g, salt 0.3g

Seared scallops with flavoured greens

The size of scallops can vary. If they are small you will need three per serving; if they are big ones from a fishmonger, halve them horizontally and serve one-and-a-half.

TAKES 20 MINUTES • SERVES 2

2 tbsp rapeseed oil
1 shallot, diced
1 small garlic clove, crushed
zest and juice ½ lemon
100g/4oz dark greens, such as
    cavalo nero or kale, stalks removed
    then shredded
1 tbsp chopped anchovies
3 scallops, roe removed and halved
    horizontally
knob of butter

1 Heat half of the oil in a frying pan. Add the shallots, garlic and lemon zest, and fry gently until soft. Add the greens and the anchovies, and cook for 5 minutes until the leaves are wilted.

2 Meanwhile, heat the remaining oil in a non-stick pan, then add the scallops and fry for 1–2 minutes on each side. Add the butter and lemon juice to the pan and swirl until the butter melts and you have a glossy sauce. Divide the greens and scallops between 2 plates and serve with the pan juices spooned over.

PER SERVING 146 kcals, protein 18g, carbs 1g, fat 8g, sat fat 2g, fibre 2g, sugar 1g, salt 1.33g

Griddled asparagus with flaked almonds & lemony butter

Despite its simplicity the combination of buttery almonds and asparagus is truly divine.

TAKES 20 MINUTES • **SERVES 2**

200g/7oz asparagus spears
drizzle olive oil
1 tbsp flaked almonds
25g/1oz butter
good squeeze lemon juice

1 Cook the asparagus spears in lots of boiling salted water for about 2–3 minutes, you want them to be tender but still with a little bite. Drain them well and toss with a little olive oil and a good pinch of salt and pepper.

2 Heat a griddle pan to very hot, place the spears on the griddle and cook for a few minutes, turning to get a nice charred effect all over.

3 Meanwhile heat a small pan and toast the nuts for about 45 seconds, until they start to turn golden – you will be able to smell when they are toasted. Tip out and set aside. Add the butter and gently melt, then add the lemon and take off the heat. Divide the asparagus between two plates and top each pile with a drizzle of melted butter and the toasted almonds.

PER SERVING 107 kcals, protein 4g, carbs 3g, fat 9g, sat fat 3g, fibre 2g, sugar 2g, salt 0.1g

Steak salad with blue cheese vinaigrette

Give steak a superhealthy makeover with this special supper for two.

TAKES 25 MINUTES • SERVES 2

1 fillet or rump steak (about
    300g/10oz), trimmed
140g/5oz green beans, trimmed
1 head chicory, leaves separated
25g/1oz walnuts, roughly chopped

FOR THE DRESSING

zest and juice ½ lemon
1 tbsp walnut or olive oil
1 tbsp chopped tarragon (optional)
1 small shallot, finely chopped
1 tbsp blue cheese, crumbled

1 Season the steak with lots of pepper
and a little salt. Pan fry or cook under
the grill for 2–3 minutes each side for
medium–rare, or to your liking. Let it
sit for 10 minutes, then cut into slices.
Set aside.

2 For the dressing, in a small bowl, whisk
together the lemon zest and juice, oil,
tarragon (if using), shallot, cheese and
some salt and pepper. Set aside.

3 Cook the beans in boiling water until
just tender. Drain and rinse under cold
water, then drain thoroughly.

4 Divide the chicory leaves between two
plates and top with the beans, walnuts
and steak slices. Pour the dressing over
the salad just before eating.

PER SERVING 390 kcals, protein 38g, carbs 5g,
fat 24g, sat fat 5g, fibre 3g, sugar 3g, salt 0.42g

Marinated beetroot with grilled goat's cheese

Earthy beetroot works perfectly with creamy goat's cheese for an easy but impressive starter.

TAKES 15 MINUTES, PLUS MARINATING • SERVES 2

3 tbsp olive oil, plus extra for greasing
1½ tbsp red wine vinegar
½ tsp sugar
½ tsp thyme leaves
2 raw beetroots, peeled and very thinly sliced
100g vegetarian goat's cheese round with rind, halved horizontally
2 handfuls rocket leaves

1 Mix the oil, vinegar, sugar and thyme in a shallow dish and season well. Add the sliced beetroot and marinate for at least 1 hour or overnight, if you have time.
2 Heat grill to high. Season the goat's cheese slices, then put them on an oiled baking sheet and grill for 2–3 minutes until golden and melting.
3 Lift out the beetroot, reserving the marinade, and divide between two plates. Top with most of the rocket, a round of goat's cheese then the remaining rocket. Drizzle with the marinade and serve.

PER SERVING 293 kcals, protein 9g, carbs 10g, fat 25g, sat fat 8g, fibre 2g, sugar 9g, salt 0.77g

Seared beef salad

If you want to serve this to vegetarians, leave out the beef and use sliced roasted red peppers from a jar instead.

TAKES 30 MINUTES • SERVES 2

1 red onion, cut through the root into 6 wedges
1 tbsp olive oil, plus extra for drizzling
½ tsp thyme leaves
1 tsp balsamic vinegar
2 handfuls mixed salad leaves
140g/5oz beef fillet, cut into 6 thin slices
25g/1oz blue cheese, roughly crumbled

FOR THE DRESSING

1½ tbsp olive oil
1 tsp balsamic vinegar
1 tsp Dijon mustard

1 Heat oven to 220C/200C fan/gas 7. Put the onion in a roasting tin, drizzle with the olive oil and sprinkle over the thyme. Season and roast in the oven for 15–20 minutes or until tender and caramelised at the edges. Remove from the oven and sprinkle over the balsamic vinegar.

2 While the onions are cooking, make the dressing by mixing all the ingredients together with some seasoning.

3 Just before the onions have finished cooking, put a griddle pan or frying pan on a high heat and, while the pan heats up, toss the salad leaves in the dressing and divide between plates.

4 Drizzle the beef with a little extra olive oil and season with salt and pepper; then, when the pan is very hot, add the meat and cook for about 30 seconds on each side (or longer, if you prefer). Once the beef is cooked to your liking, put three slices on each plate next to the salad, along with three wedges of roasted red onion. Finally, scatter over the blue cheese and serve.

PER SERVING 338 kcals, protein 19g, carbs 6g, fat 26g, sat fat 7g, fibre 1g, sugar 5g, salt 0.8g

Whipped Brie with dates & candied walnuts

Sweet nuts and creamy Brie are a perfect combination – you could also try this with a soft goat's cheese too.

TAKES 25 MINUTES ● SERVES 2

140g/5oz ripe Brie, rind removed
25g/1oz stoned dates, cut into small
   pieces
two handfuls rocket leaves
25g/1oz shop-bought croutons,
   crumbled

FOR THE CANDIED WALNUTS

25g/1oz walnuts, halved
2 tsp caster sugar

FOR THE DRESSING

3 tbsp walnut oil
1 tbsp balsamic vinegar

1 Heat oven to 190C/170C fan/gas 5. To make the candied walnuts, shake the walnut halves in 1 teaspoon water, then toss in the sugar. Scatter over a baking sheet and bake in the oven for 6–8 minutes until golden brown. Remove from the oven and allow to cool.

2 Put the Brie in a medium-sized bowl. Using a spoon or small whisk, whip the cheese until pale and spoonable. Set aside.

3 To make the dressing, whisk the oil and vinegar together, then season.

4 In a large bowl, combine the walnuts, dates and rocket, then mix with some of the dressing. Put a spoonful of whipped Brie in the middle of each serving plate and arrange the salad around it. Scatter over the croutons, drizzle with a little extra dressing and serve.

PER SERVING 587 kcals, protein 19g, carbs 22g, fat 46g, sat fat 15g, fibre 2g, sugar 13g, salt 1.23g

Mustard pork fillet with apple lentils & herb aïoli

Pork loin fillets are fairly inexpensive and yet look elegant at a dinner party.

TAKES 35 MINUTES ● SERVES 2

350g/12oz pork loin fillet
1 tbsp olive oil
1 tbsp Dijon mustard
small bunch tarragon, chopped
100g/4oz Puy lentils
350ml/12fl oz vegetable stock
zest and juice ⅓ lemon
½ small apple, cored and diced
85g/3oz good-quality mayonnaise
1 small garlic clove, crushed
green beans, steamed, to serve

1 Heat oven to 200C/180C fan/gas 6. Rub the pork with the oil and some seasoning, then brown the outside of the meat all over in a hot frying pan. Transfer the pork to a baking sheet, brush the outside with the mustard, then press on half of the tarragon and cook for 20 minutes. Remove from the oven, cover with foil and rest for 5 minutes.

2 Meanwhile, cook the lentils in the stock until just tender, about 12 minutes. Drain, then toss with half the lemon juice and the apple.

3 To make the aïoli, mix the mayonnaise, garlic, lemon zest and remaining juice and tarragon with some seasoning in a small bowl. Slice the pork into thick slices and serve on a platter with the lentils, a bowl of aïoli to dip into and some steamed green beans.

PER SERVING 782 kcals, protein 55g, carbs 30g, fat 49g, sat fat 9g, fibre 6g, sugar 5g, salt 2g

Slow-roast belly of pork

This simple recipe proves that if you buy the best-quality meat, you need do nothing more to it than season and roast, and the natural flavours will speak for themselves.

TAKES 2 HOURS AND 10 MINUTES, PLUS RESTING • SERVES 2

500g/1lb 2oz pork belly, scored
1 tbsp butter
1 tbsp flour
250ml/9fl oz chicken stock
wilted greens, pickled beetroot and roast potatoes, to serve

1 Heat oven to 180C/160C fan/gas 4. Put the pork on a wire rack in a roasting tin, skin-side up, and cook for 30 minutes. Increase the oven temperature to 220C/200C fan/gas 7 and cook for a further 15–20 minutes to crisp the skin. Remove the pork from the tin and allow to rest for 15 minutes.
2 To make the gravy, remove all the fat from the bottom of the roasting tin. Add the butter and heat to melt. Tip in the flour and cook for 1–2 minutes, scraping the bottom of the pan. Gradually stir in the stock and cook for 5 minutes until thick. Serve with wilted greens, some pickled beetroot and roast potatoes.

PER SERVING 575 kcals, protein 45g, carbs 7.4g, fat 41g, sat fat 16g, fibre 0.9g, sugar 0.3g, salt 0.8g

One-pan duck with Savoy cabbage

Duck breast is perfect for entertaining – it's easy to cook, readily available, yet not something you eat every day.

TAKES 40 MINUTES • SERVES 2

1 duck breast
½ tsp black peppercorns, crushed
300g/10oz cooked new potatoes, thickly sliced
small bunch flat-leaf parsley, roughly chopped
1 garlic clove, finely chopped
3 rashers smoked streaky bacon, chopped
½ Savoy cabbage, trimmed, quartered, cored and finely sliced
½ tbsp balsamic vinegar
1 tbsp olive oil

1 Lightly score the skin of the duck breast and season with the peppercorns and some salt. Lay the duck breast, skin-side down, in a non-stick sauté pan, then put over a low heat. Leave the duck to cook for 15 minutes, then flip over on to the flesh side for 5 minutes.

2 Remove the duck from the pan, then turn up the heat. Add the potatoes to the pan, fry until brown and crisp, then scatter over the parsley and garlic. Scoop out on to a plate, then season with salt.

3 Keep the pan on the heat. Fry the bacon until crisp, then add the cabbage. Cook for 1 minute, add a splash of water, then fry for 2 minutes, just until the cabbage is wilted. While the cabbage is cooking, whisk any juices from the duck with the vinegar and olive oil to make a dressing.

4 Carve the duck breast into slices. Fan out on large dinner plates, spoon a neat bundle of cabbage on one side, then pile a serving of potatoes on the other. Drizzle over the dressing and serve.

PER SERVING 518 kcals, protein 22g, carbs 28g, fat 35g, sat fat 9g, fibre 6g, sugar 7g, salt 1.2g

Lemon sole with crab & tarragon butter sauce

This impressive fish dish looks great on a platter for sharing – just add buttery new potatoes and some greens, if you like.

TAKES 40 MINUTES ● SERVES 2

50g/2oz butter, softened
1 tbsp chopped tarragon leaves
50g/2oz crab, half white meat, half brown
1 lemon, zest removed, then cut into thin slices
1 large whole lemon sole or 2 small ones, descaled and gutted (ask your fishmonger to do this), washed and dried
50ml/2fl oz white wine
1 tbsp capers, rinsed and drained
2 tbsp double cream
steamed potatoes and green salad, to serve

1 Heat oven to 200C/180C fan/gas 6. In a small bowl, mash the butter with the tarragon, crabmeat and lemon zest. Season.

2 Make a few deep slashes across the fillets on both sides of the sole, then put the fish, dark-skin side up, in a roasting tin. Season, then stuff the crab butter into the cuts, spreading any remaining butter on top. Lay a few lemon slices over the fish, then pour over the wine.

3 Bake for 15–20 minutes, depending on the size of the fish – the flesh should flake away easily from the bone when gently pushed with a knife.

4 Carefully remove the fish from the tin, put on a warm plate or platter and cover with foil. Set the tin over a low heat, add 2 tablespoons water and bring to the boil. Let it bubble for a few minutes, then stir in the capers and cream. Pour the sauce over the fish and serve with steamed potatoes and a green salad.

PER SERVING 492 kcals, protein 27g, carbs 2g, fat 40g, sat fat 24g, fibre none, sugar 2g, salt 1.3g

Grilled dab with garlic butter

Dab is a sustainable flat fish similar to sole or plaice – it's delicious simply grilled and served with garlic butter.

TAKES 30 MINUTES ● SERVES 2

4 whole dabs, dark skin scored
1 tbsp olive oil
50g/2oz butter
2 garlic cloves, thinly sliced
juice ½ lemon
small bunch flat-leaf parsley, finely
    chopped
250g/8oz baby spinach leaves

1 Heat grill to high. Cut the frills away from the sides of the dabs using scissors. Lay the fish on a baking sheet, dark-skin side up, drizzle with a little olive oil and sprinkle with some sea salt. Put under a hot grill for 5 minutes, until cooked through and the flesh comes away from the bone when prodded.

2 Meanwhile, heat the butter in a frying pan until it starts to turn brown, then add the garlic and cook until it just starts to change colour. Remove the pan from the heat, add the lemon juice and parsley, stir together. Set aside and keep warm.

3 Wilt the spinach in a colander by pouring over a kettle of boiling water, then divide between two plates. Put two dabs on top of the spinach on each plate, drizzle with the butter sauce and serve.

PER SERVING 643 kcals, protein 83g, carbs 3g, fat 33g, sat fat 14g, fibre 3g, sugar 2g, salt 1.8g

Tandoori-spiced sea bream

Simple to prep but with pretty special results, this Indian-inspired main course makes a romantic meal for two.

TAKES 30 MINUTES, PLUS CHILLING
● **SERVES 2**
olive oil, for frying
2 sea bream fillets
new potatoes with saffron-infused butter and green beans stir-fried with mustard seeds and desiccated coconut, to serve (optional)

FOR THE TANDOORI BUTTER
1 tsp garlic paste
1 tsp ginger paste
2 green chillies
¼ tsp red chilli powder
½ tsp ground turmeric
½ tsp garam masala
juice ½ lime
100g/4oz unsalted butter

1 Mix the tandoori butter ingredients, plus some seasoning, in a small food processor or by hand until smooth. Scrape on to a sheet of cling film in a strip, then use the cling film to help roll the butter into a cylinder shape. Twist the ends to seal in the butter log and chill until firm. The butter will last in the fridge for a week, or in the freezer for up to 3 months.

2 Heat a heavy-based frying pan with a drizzle of oil until really hot. Season the fish, then put in the pan, skin-side down, and cook for 4–5 minutes until crisp and almost cooked through. Carefully turn over, add a good tablespoon of tandoori butter to the pan and spoon it over the fish as it melts. Serve straight away with saffron new potatoes and spiced green beans, if you like.

PER SERVING 225 kcals, protein 26g, carbs none, fat 13g, sat fat 5g, fibre none, sugar none, salt 0.42g

Salted caramel choc pots

Something sweet just for two – these puds are simple enough for anyone to make, but unbelievably good!

TAKES 35 MINUTES, PLUS CHILLING
- **SERVES 2**

4 tbsp dulce de leche or canned caramel
½ tsp sea salt, plus extra to scatter
85g/3oz each dark and milk chocolate, broken into squares
1–2 long thin plain grissini (bread sticks)
2 tbsp demerara sugar
100ml/3½fl oz double cream, at room temperature
50ml/2fl oz milk

1 Mix the caramel with the salt, divide between two small glasses and chill.

2 Melt the chocolates together in a glass bowl set over a pan of barely simmering water. Snap the grissini into short lengths, then dip each end into the chocolate to coat a little. Sit on a wire rack for the chocolate to drip and set a little, then dip the chocolate ends into the sugar to coat. Sit in an airtight container lined with baking parchment and chill until ready to serve.

3 Stir the double cream and milk into the remaining melted chocolate until smooth, then scrape into a jug. Slowly pour on top of the caramel, around the edges first. Chill the pots for at least 2 hours, or up to 24 hours.

4 To serve, scatter a little more sea salt on top of each pot, then add one or two sugar-tipped grissini.

PER SERVING 847 kcals, protein 8g, carbs 83g, fat 53g, sat fat 32g, fibre 2g, sugar 79g, salt 1.5g

Clementine & Grand Marnier semifreddos

Although this recipe makes six semifreddos it is worth making the full quantity and keeping them in the freezer to have another time.

TAKES 1 HOUR 5 MINUTES

● **MAKES 6**

2 clementines, 6 unpeeled slices, the rest peeled and thinly sliced
50g/2oz caster sugar
sunflower oil, for greasing
2 tbsp Grand Marnier liqueur
2 tbsp shredless marmalade

FOR THE SEMIFREDDOS

3 large eggs, separated
85g/3oz caster sugar
270ml pot double cream

1 Put the peeled and sliced clementines in a pan with the sugar and 300ml/½ pint water. Cover and simmer for 20 minutes, then add the Grand Marnier. Cool.

2 Meanwhile, oil and line six baby pudding or dariole moulds with cling film.

3 Add the marmalade to the syrup and boil until it has reduced to about 6 tablespoons. Put 1 tablespoon of the marmalade syrup into the base of each mould; put a clementine slice on top.

4 Beat the egg whites until stiff with an electric whisk. Add the sugar to the egg yolks; whisk until thick and leaving a trail. Beat the cream until it holds its shape.

5 Stir the yolks into the cream, then fold in the whites. Spoon on top of the clementines. If you want to freeze them, put the pots straight into the freezer. When solid, wrap with cling film, then foil.

6 To serve, remove from the moulds and turn out into small coupe glasses.

PER SERVING 426 kcals, protein 5g, carbs 31g, fat 31g, sat fat 16g, fibre none, sugar 31g, salt 0.15g

Salted caramel banana Tatins

When there's just two of you a banana Tatin is the perfect indulgent treat.

TAKES 55 MINUTES, PLUS CHILLING
● **SERVES 2**

250g/9oz ready-made puff pastry
plain flour, for dusting
1 banana, peeled
50g/2oz light brown soft sugar
50g/2oz butter
2 tbsp double cream
½ tsp sea salt flakes, plus extra
  to sprinkle
2 scoops vanilla ice cream to serve

1 To make the Tatins, roll out the pastry on a floured surface to the thickness of a £1 coin. Cut out two lids big enough to fit over the banana, leaving a 1cm/½in border. Put on a baking tray and chill in the fridge for fifteen minutes.

2 Set a heavy-bottomed, ovenproof frying pan over a medium heat. Add the sugar, butter and cream, and cook for 5 minutes until the sugar has melted and the caramel is bubbling. Add the sea salt flakes. Slice the banana in half lengthways and put the two halves, cut-side down, into the caramel.

3 Heat oven to 220C/200C fan/gas 7. Put a pastry lid on top of each banana half, tucking each in tightly around the edges. Transfer the pan to the oven and cook for 20 minutes until the pastry is risen and golden. Quickly turn out the Tatins, sprinkle with the extra sea salt flakes and serve with scoops of ice cream.

PER SERVING 940 kcals, protein 8g, carbs 78g, fat 66g, sat fat 37g, fibre 0.8g, sugar 36g, salt 2.9g

Coffee cocktails & star biscuits

An indulgent creamy coffee becomes an after-dinner star. The recipe makes about 40 biscuits, but they will freeze well or keep in an airtight container for up to 3 days.

TAKES 40 MINUTES, PLUS CHILLING
- **MAKES 2 DRINKS AND 40 BISCUITS**

FOR THE BISCUITS

200g/7oz very soft butter
140g/5oz caster sugar
1 egg yolk
1 tsp vanilla extract
300g/10oz plain flour, plus a little
  extra for rolling
icing sugar, for dusting

FOR THE COCKTAILS

100ml/4fl oz strong coffee, cooled
2 tbsp Kahlúa coffee liqueur
4 tbsp double cream
cocoa powder, for dusting
chocolate truffles, to serve (optional)

1 Mix together the butter, sugar, egg yolk and vanilla using a wooden spoon. Stir in the flour. Tip on to a floured surface and bring together into a smooth dough.

2 Roll out the dough and stamp out 5–6cm/2–2¼in stars. Keep re-rolling the trimmings – you should get about 40 biscuits. Cut out a thin triangle about 2cm/¾in long and ½cm/¼in wide at one of the indents of each star. Arrange on baking sheets lined with parchment, cover with cling film. Chill for 30 minutes.

3 Heat oven to 200C/180C fan/ gas 6. Remove cling film and bake the biscuits for 8–12 minutes until golden. Cool, dust with icing sugar, then serve slotted on to the edge of glasses. The cooked biscuits can be frozen for up to 3 months.

4 Mix the coffee and Kahlúa in a jug and divide between two Martini glasses. Slowly pour in the double cream over the back of a teaspoon so that it settles on the top of each coffee. Dust with a little cocoa and serve with some truffles.

PER SERVING 78 kcals, protein 1g, carbs 9g, fat 4g, sat fat 3g, fibre none, sugar 4g, salt 0.06g

Frozen lychee & mint cocktails

This recipe makes enough for two each. You can replace the vodka with lychee juice for a non-alcoholic version. Delicious with prawn crackers and a dipping sauce.

TAKES 10 MINUTES • SERVES 2

400g can lychees in syrup
small bunch mint, 2 sprigs reserved to
    garnish
100ml/3½fl oz vodka
juice 2 limes
2 handfuls ice

1 Open the can of lychees and drain the syrup into a blender. Add four of the lychees, the mint leaves, vodka and lime juice. Add the ice and blend until slushy. Serve in glasses garnished with a mint sprig and a lychee.

PER SERVING 98 kcals, protein none, carbs 11g, fat none, sat fat none, fibre none, sugar 11g, salt none

Mini smoked haddock Scotch eggs with asparagus dippers & watercress mayonnaise

All of this can be assembled the day before. If you have kids around, this is a great dish for them to help out with.

TAKES 1 HOUR 25 MINUTES, PLUS CHILLING • SERVES 8

16 asparagus spears, trimmed

FOR THE SCOTCH EGGS

400g/14oz potatoes, cut into chunks
400g/14oz skinned smoked haddock, cut into large chunks
16 quail's eggs
25g/1oz butter
2 tbsp milk
50g/2oz plain flour
2 eggs, beaten
100g/4oz breadcrumbs
sunflower oil, for frying

FOR THE WATERCRESS MAYONNAISE

100g bag watercress
1 tbsp lemon juice
150ml/¼ pint mayonnaise

1 For the Scotch eggs, tip the potatoes into a pan; cover with water. Bring to the boil, then tip in the haddock and quail's eggs. Cook the eggs for 2 minutes, then remove them. Cool under cold running water. Continue cooking the haddock until it flakes, and the potatoes until soft. Drain; mash with the butter and milk until you have a thick mash. Set aside to cool.

2 Meanwhile, peel the eggs. Pat out spoonfuls of mash mix and mould them around the eggs. Roll the covered eggs in the flour, then the beaten egg, then breadcrumbs. Chill for 1 hour to firm up.

3 For the mayonnaise, blitz the watercress with the lemon juice until finely chopped, then stir through the mayonnaise. Blanch the asparagus for 4 minutes, then drain under cold water.

4 To serve, heat sunflower oil in a frying pan. Fry the eggs until crisp on all sides, then drain on kitchen paper. Serve with the asparagus and mayonnaise.

PER SERVING 370 kcals, protein 18g, carbs 23g, fat 23g, sat fat 5g, fibre 2g, sugar 2g, salt 1.5g

Prawn cocktail crostini

You can make the sauce the day before and then just assemble the crostini on the day of your dinner party.

TAKES 25 MINUTES ● MAKES 8

2 ripe avocados
1 tbsp lemon juice
300g/10oz cooked and peeled tiger
  prawns
2 tbsp olive oil
1 large ciabatta, diagonally cut into
  8 slices
8 nice Baby Gem leaves
cayenne pepper and lemon wedges,
  to garnish and squeeze over

FOR THE COCKTAIL SAUCE

6 tbsp mayonnaise
2 tbsp tomato ketchup
2 tsp brandy (optional)
few drops Tabasco sauce

1 To make the sauce, mix all ingredients in a bowl, season well and set to one side. If you're making this the day before, cover and put in the fridge until needed.
2 Peel, then chop the avocados into small chunks, tossing in lemon juice as you go, so they don't discolour.
3 Mix the prawns with half the sauce, add the avocados and stir gently to coat everything.
4 Heat a griddle pan. To make the crostini, rub a little olive oil on to each slice of ciabatta and griddle on each side for 2 minutes until toasted.
5 To serve, spread a little of the reserved cocktail sauce on each crostini, top with a lettuce leaf and add a spoonful of the prawn cocktail mix. Sprinkle with a little cayenne pepper and serve with lemon wedges.

PER CROSTINI 315 kcals, protein 13g, carbs 21g, fat 20g, sat fat 4g, fibre 2g, sugar 3g, salt 1.46g

Smoky aubergine & coriander dip

The seductively smoky flavour of this Middle Eastern-style dip comes from cooking the aubergines to charcoal black.

TAKES 45 MINUTES, PLUS COOLING
- **SERVES 10**

4 large aubergines
4 tbsp Greek yogurt
2 tbsp olive oil
large bunch coriander, leaves only, finely chopped
1 garlic clove, crushed
squeeze lemon or lime juice
crispbreads or toasted pitta bread, to serve

1 Light the gas on two rings, then lay the aubergines directly on them, two to a ring. In 30 seconds they will have blackened on one side, so use tongs to turn them until they are well charred on all sides. Alternatively, cook them under the grill or on the barbecue, turning them until they are blackened all over.

2 Once done, put the aubergines in a plastic bag. When cool enough to handle, strip away the blackened skin and put the flesh (which should be cooked and soft) in a colander to drain for 30 minutes.

3 Transfer the aubergine to a bowl, then mash with a fork or blitz with a hand-held blender, but don't make it completely smooth. Stir in the yogurt, olive oil and a fat pinch of salt, then add the coriander, garlic and lemon or lime juice. Taste and add more salt or juice if necessary, but be careful not to overwhelm the aubergine flavour. Serve with crispbread or toasted pitta breads.

PER SERVING 49 kcals, protein 2g, carbs 3g, fat 3g, sat fat 1g, fibre 3g, sugar 3g, salt 0.02g

Tomato, feta & pesto bites

Think of these as bites rather than canapés – they're more informal and a lot less fiddly.

TAKES 1½ HOURS, PLUS CHILLING
- **MAKES 12**

½ × 350g pack puff pastry (freeze
    the rest to use another time)
25g/1oz finely grated Parmesan
20g pack basil
2 tbsp pine nuts
100g/4oz feta, crumbled
1 garlic clove, crushed
4 tbsp olive oil
12 small cherry tomatoes, halved
parsley leaves, to garnish

1 Roll out the pastry on a surface dusted with the Parmesan to about the thickness of a 10-pence piece. Stamp out 12 rounds using a 6cm plain cutter and line a shallow 12-hole bun tin. Chill for 20 minutes.
2 Heat oven to 200C/180C fan/gas 6. Prick each pastry base with a fork and bake for 15–20 minutes until golden. Remove from the tin and leave to cool on a wire rack.
3 Meanwhile, put the basil leaves in a food processor with the pine nuts, then whizz until coarsely chopped. Then add the feta, garlic and oil, and whizz to make a thick paste. The pastry bases will keep in a tin for up to 2 days and the pesto will keep in the fridge overnight.
4 Dollop a spoonful of the feta pesto on to the pastry tarts to serve and top each one with two cherry tomato halves. Garnish with the parsley leaves.

PER BITE 271 kcals, protein 7g, carbs 11g, fat 22g, sat fat 8g, fibre none, sugar 1.2g, salt 0.96g

Lemony prawns & avocado

Serve these starters in glasses so you can see the lovely layers of colour. You can make them up to 2 hours ahead of serving.

TAKES 25 MINUTES • SERVES 12

4 ripe avocados, chopped into small
  chunks
juice 2 lemons or 4 limes
12 cherry tomatoes, chopped
4 tbsp snipped chives
good dash Tabasco sauce
600g/1lb 5oz large peeled, cooked
  prawns, defrosted and patted dry
  if frozen
300g/10oz fromage frais
2 baguettes, sliced
olive oil, for brushing

1 Mix the avocado in a bowl with the lemon or lime juice. Add the tomatoes to the bowl with 2 tablespoons of the chives and the Tabasco, then season to taste.

2 Divide the prawns among 12 glasses or glass dishes. Spoon over the avocado mixture. Mix the fromage frais with 1 tablespoon of the chives, then season to taste. Spoon onto the avocado mix, then sprinkle with the remaining chives. You can now chill for up to 2 hours before serving.

3 Brush the baguette slices with olive oil and toast under the grill to serve alongside.

PER GLASS 350 kcals, protein 18g, carbs 26g, fat 20g, sat fat 4g, fibre 3g, sugar 3g, salt 1.58g

Halloumi-stuffed peppers

This dish also doubles up as a starter for eight. Serve half a pepper per person with a few dressed salad leaves on the side.

TAKES 55 MINUTES • SERVES 4

4 large red peppers
290g jar antipasti marinated
    mushrooms
50g/2oz couscous
100ml/3½fl oz hot vegetable stock
250g/9oz halloumi, cut into cubes
2 tbsp chopped parsley
mixed salad and garlic bread, to serve

1 Heat oven to 200C/180C fan/gas 6. Cut the peppers in half through the stalks and scoop out the seeds. Put the peppers in one layer on a baking sheet. Drain the mushrooms, reserving the oil from the jar – drizzle 1 tablespoon of the oil over the peppers, then sprinkle with salt and pepper. Bake for 20–25 minutes, until the peppers are just tender.

2 Tip the couscous into a bowl and pour in the hot stock. Leave for 5 minutes to soak, then fluff up with a fork and stir in the mushrooms, halloumi and parsley. Season with salt and pepper and spoon into the pepper halves. Return to the oven for 15 minutes, until the cheese is golden. Serve warm with a mixed salad and garlic bread.

PER SERVING 334 kcals, protein 16g, carbs 19g, fat 22g, sat fat 10g, fibre 4g, sugar 10.5g, salt 2.4g

Sea bass & seafood Italian one-pot

Just put this dish in the middle of the table, lift off the lid and your guests will realise impressive food doesn't have to be fussy or fancy.

TAKES 1 HOUR • SERVES 4

2 tbsp olive oil
1 fennel bulb, halved and sliced, fronds kept separate to garnish
2 garlic cloves, sliced
½ red chilli, chopped
250g/9oz cleaned squid, sliced into rings
bunch basil, leaves and stalks separated, stalks tied together, leaves roughly chopped
400g can chopped tomatoes
150ml/¼ pint white wine
2 large handfuls mussels or clams
8 large raw prawns (whole look nicest)
4 sea bass fillets (about 140g/5oz each)
crusty bread, to serve

1 Heat the oil in a large pan with a tight-fitting lid, then add the fennel, garlic and chilli. Fry until softened, then add the squid, basil stalks, tomatoes and wine. Simmer over a low heat for 35 minutes until the squid is tender and the sauce has thickened slightly, then season.

2 Scatter the mussels or clams and prawns over the sauce, lay the sea bass fillets on top, cover, turn up the heat and cook hard for 5 minutes. Serve scattered with the basil leaves and fennel fronds, with crusty bread alongside.

PER SERVING 329 kcals, protein 45g, carbs 7g, fat 11g, sat fat 2g, fibre 2g, sugar 4g, salt 1g

One-pot chicken and chorizo with rice

This one-pot is full of flavour from the chorizo sausage, just serve with some crusty bread.

TAKES 1 HOUR 40 MINUTES

● **SERVES 6**

1 tbsp oil
8 chicken pieces or 1 large whole
  chicken, jointed
1 large onion, chopped
1 red pepper, deseeded and chopped
  into large chunks
3 garlic cloves, crushed
225g/8oz chorizo, skinned and sliced
1 tbsp tomato purée
1 tbsp thyme leaves, chopped
150ml/¼pint white wine
850ml/1½pints chicken or vegetable
  stock
400g/14oz long-grain rice
2 tbsp chopped parsley

1 Heat the oil in a large flameproof casserole and brown the chicken pieces all over – you may have to do this in batches unless you have a really large pan. Remove from the dish once browned and set aside.

2 Turn down the heat, add the onion and pepper, and gently cook fry for 10 minutes until softened. Add the garlic and chorizo, and cook for a further 2 minutes until the chorizo starts to crisp, then add the puree and stir to combine.

3 Return the chicken with the thyme, white wine and stock. Bring to the boil, cover with a tight-fitting lid and turn down to a gentle simmer. Cook for 30 mins, then add the rice, mix well and cover. Cook for about 15 mins more, until the rice is tender.

4 Take off the heat and stand with the lid on for 15 mins, then season and scatter with the parsley before serving.

PER SERVING 834 kcals, protein 63g, carbs 90g, fat 21g, sat fat 7g, fibre 4g, sugar 9g, salt 1.7g

Mediterranean fish stew with garlic toasts

Feed a crowd of friends like a Mediterranean mamma, with this gloriously summery seafood stew.

TAKES 1 HOUR 25 MINUTES

● **SERVES 8**

3 tbsp olive oil
1 large onion, sliced
2 garlic cloves, sliced
1 red chilli, finely chopped
2 tbsp tomato purée
1kg/2lb 4oz tomatoes, roughly chopped
200ml/7fl oz white wine
350ml/12fl oz fish stock
3 strips orange zest
1kg/2lb 4oz skinless halibut fillets, cut
   into large chunks
500g/1lb 2oz clams
400g/14oz large raw prawns
handful flat-leaf parsley, chopped

FOR THE GARLIC TOASTS

1 large ciabatta loaf, cut into 1cm/½in
   slices
5 tbsp olive oil
2 garlic cloves, halved

1 To make the garlic toasts, drizzle the bread with oil, then griddle or grill until golden all over. While the toasts are still hot, rub them with garlic and set aside.

2 Heat the oil in a wide, deep frying pan. Add the onion and cook over a gentle heat for 5 minutes until softened. Stir through the garlic and chilli, and cook for a couple of minutes more. Add the tomato purée and tomatoes. Turn up the heat and cook for 10–15 minutes, stirring until the tomatoes are pulpy. Pour over the wine and cook for 10 minutes more until most of it has boiled away.

3 Add the fish stock and orange zest, and heat until gently simmering. Nestle the halibut chunks into the liquid and cook for 5 minutes. Add the clams and prawns, and cook for 5 minutes more until the fish is cooked through and the clams have opened (discard any that haven't). Sprinkle the parsley over the stew and serve with the garlic toasts.

PER SERVING 411 kcals, protein 39g, carbs 28g, fat 16g, sat fat 2g, fibre 3g, sugar 8g, salt 1.17g

Seared chicken & asparagus with mango salsa

This recipe is perfect for feeding a crowd, but is easily halved too. Make the salsa the day before and keep it in the fridge until you need it.

TAKES 55 MINUTES ● SERVES 10

FOR THE MANGO SALSA

2 medium firm but ripe mangoes, peeled and finely diced

juice 1 lime, zest ½

1 small red onion, finely chopped

2 red chillies, deseeded and finely chopped

small bunch each flat-leaf parsley and coriander, chopped

125ml/4fl oz extra virgin olive oil

1 tsp caster sugar (optional)

FOR THE ASPARAGUS

30 asparagus spears, tough ends snapped off

50ml/2fl oz olive oil

FOR THE CHICKEN

10 skinless boneless chicken breasts (about 140g/5oz each)

3 tbsp olive oil

1 To make the mango salsa, put the mango into a bowl with the lime juice and zest, red onion, chillies, parsley, coriander and olive oil. Taste, and mix in a teaspoon of sugar, if you feel it needs it.

2 Heat the oven to 200C/180C fan/gas 6. Put two baking sheets in the oven to preheat. Toss the asparagus in the olive oil and season with salt and pepper.

3 Roast the aasparagus on the preheated baking sheets for 12–14 minutes, shaking them halfway through. When cooked, remove the asparagus from the baking sheets to cool. Leave the oven on.

4 For the chicken, heat a griddle pan over a high heat until hot. Brush the chicken with olive oil and season with salt and pepper. Cook the chicken breasts in the pan for 2–3 minutes each side. Remove from the griddle and lay on foil-lined baking sheets. Roast for 12–15 minutes. Serve on top of the asparagus with a dollop of salsa.

PER SERVING 379 kcals, protein 35g, carbs 8g, fat 22g, sat fat 3.5g, fibre 2g, sugar 7.5g, salt 0.2g

Steak & clever chips

These are clever chips because they don't involve three stages of cooking and thermometers – the method used by many smart restaurants – but still taste as good.

TAKES 50 MINUTES, PLUS CHILLING

● **SERVES 2**

600g/1lb 5oz medium-sized King Edward or Maris Piper potatoes

sunflower oil, for frying

2 × 200g/7oz beef steaks

2 handfuls mixed salad leaves

dressing of your choice, to serve

FOR THE BUTTER

50g/2oz butter, softened

small handful parsley leaves, finely chopped

1 small garlic clove, minced (optional)

small squeeze lemon juice

1 To make the butter: mash all the ingredients together with lots of cracked black pepper. Pat the butter flat between cling film. Put in the fridge to harden.

2 Cut the potatoes into chips, rinse under hot water, then dry on a tea towel. Put the chips in a deep pan and just cover with oil. Put the pan on a medium heat, bring to a simmer and give the chips a stir with a wooden spoon. Increase the heat so the oil bubbles really quickly and fry the chips, stirring occasionally so they don't stick, until crisp and golden. When they are done, scoop out on to a plate lined with kitchen paper and set aside.

3 Meanwhile, heat a griddle pan until really hot. Season the steaks with salt and pepper, and rub with a little oil. For a steak that's 2cm/¾in thick, cook it for 2 minutes on each side for rare, adding 1 minute for every degree of doneness. Just before lifting the steaks off the griddle, put half the butter on top of each. Serve with the chips and dressed mixed leaves.

PER SERVING 980 kcals, protein 46g, carbs 52g, fat 67g, sat fat 25g, fibre 5g, sugar 2g, salt 0.66g

Mussels, bacon & Brie tartlets

These rich tartlets, made with Parmesan pastry, make a glamorous dinner party starter – perfect for a special occasion.

TAKES 1¼ HOURS, PLUS CHILLING
● **SERVES 8**

FOR THE PARMESAN PASTRY
140g/5oz butter
225g/8oz plain flour
50g/2oz freshly grated Parmesan
1 medium egg, beaten with 1 tbsp milk

FOR THE FILLING
2 tbsp olive oil
1 red onion, finely chopped
2 garlic cloves, finely chopped
100g/4oz dry cure streaky bacon or
    pancetta, cubed
4 medium eggs
300ml/12fl oz whipping or double
    cream
3 tbsp snipped chives
500g/1lb 2oz frozen cooked and shelled
    mussels, thawed and drained, or
    2kg/4lb 8oz fresh mussels, cooked
    and shelled
200g/7oz ripe Brie, rind removed, cubed
200g/7oz mixed salad leaves, to serve
2–3 tbsp bought or homemade
    vinaigrette, to serve

1 Rub the butter, flour and Parmesan together in a bowl. Add the egg mix and bring it all together into a dough. Knead lightly a few times with floured hands until smooth. Shape into a flat ball, cover in cling film and chill for at least 1 hour.

2 Heat oven to 200C/180C fan/gas 6. Roll the pastry out to the thickness of a £1 coin and line eight 10 × 3cm tartlet tins. Fill with greaseproof paper and baking beans, and bake for 10 minutes. Remove the beans and paper, then bake for 3–5 minutes. Leave to cool on a wire rack.

3 Reduce oven to 180C/160C fan/gas 4. Heat the olive oil in a frying pan and fry the onion for 3 minutes. Add the garlic and bacon. Cook for 2–3 minutes. Allow to cool slightly. Whisk the eggs and cream with the chives, then fold in the onion, bacon and mussels. Season.

4 Set the cases on a baking sheet. Spoon the mix in and scatter Brie over the top, pushing into the mix in places. Bake for 12–15 minutes. Serve with dressed leaves.

PER SERVING 642 kcals, protein 27g, carbs 26g, fat 54g, sat fat 28g, fibre 1g, sugar 2.8g, salt 1.85g

Herb & pepper crusted rib of beef

If you're planning a special dinner party then this crusted roast beef is guaranteed to wow your guests.

TAKES 2¾ HOURS • SERVES 8

1 tbsp rock salt
2 tbsp cracked black peppercorns
3 garlic cloves, crushed
small bunch rosemary, finely chopped
small bunch parsley, chopped
4 tbsp olive oil
3kg/6lb 8oz rib of beef on the bone
potato gratin and mixed vegetables,
   to serve (optional)

FOR THE GRAVY

2 onions, sliced
250ml/9fl oz red wine
400ml/14fl oz fresh beef stock

1 Heat oven to 220C/200C fan/gas 7. Mix the salt, peppercorns, garlic, rosemary, parsley and olive oil. Rub this mixture all over the beef rib then put in a roasting tin. Put in the oven and cook for 30 minutes, then turn the oven down to 160C/140C fan/gas 3 and cook for a further 1 hour 20 minutes. Remove from the oven, transfer the beef to a board, cover with foil and rest for 30 minutes before carving.

2 While the beef rests, make the gravy. Pour off all but 2 tablespoons fat from the roasting tin and reserve any juices. Fry the onions in the roasting tin over a medium heat for about 10 minutes, then add the wine, stock and reserved juices. Keep cooking for a further 10 minutes to reduce to a thick sauce, season well and serve alongside the roast beef. Serve with potato gratin and mixed vegetables, if you have room.

PER SERVING 694 kcals, protein 63g, carbs 4g, fat 46g, sat fat 20g, fibre 1g, sugar 2g, salt 1.43g

Praline meringue cake with strawberries

This cake needs to be assembled just before serving – however, the meringues can be made up to a day ahead, or even a month ahead and frozen.

TAKES 1½ HOURS, PLUS COOLING

● **SERVES 12**

FOR THE MERINGUE

175g/6oz whole almonds, toasted
6 egg whites
225g/8oz golden caster sugar
225g/8oz light muscovado sugar
1 tbsp cornflour
2 tsp white wine vinegar

TO ASSEMBLE

1kg/2lb 4oz strawberries, hulled and halved, or quartered if large
50g/2oz icing sugar, plus extra for decorating
600ml pot double cream

1 Heat oven to 140C/fan 120C/gas 1. Line two baking sheets with parchment. Whizz two-thirds of the almonds in a food-processor until chopped. Roughly chop the rest.

2 Beat the egg whites until stiff. Add the sugar in three batches. Beat the mixture back to stiff after each batch. Add the cornflour and vinegar; beat until glossy.

3 Fold in the finely chopped nuts and most of the roughly chopped, then divide the mixture between the two baking sheets into 20cm/8in circles, scatter the nuts over. Bake for 1 hour, turn the oven off and leave with the door closed until cool.

4 Puree 600g/1lb 5oz of the strawberries, sieve, then sweeten with 2 tablespoons of icing sugar. Add the rest of the sugar to the cream, whip until it just holds its shape, swirl through two-thirds of the sauce. Serve the meringues sandwiched together with half the cream, spoon the rest on top. Decorate with the remaining strawberries and dust with icing sugar.

PER SERVING 533 kcals, protein 7g, carbs 51g, fat 35g, sat fat 15g, fibre 2g, sugar 50g, salt 0.16g

Iced berry mousse cake

A frozen dessert is always useful when entertaining – just remember to take it out of the freezer about 40 minutes – 1 hour before serving so it defrosts enough to cut.

TAKES 50 MINUTES, PLUS FREEZING
● **SERVES 12**

FOR THE SPONGE

100g/4oz butter, softened
100g/4oz caster sugar
100g/4oz self-raising flour
¾ tsp baking powder
1 tsp vanilla extract
2 eggs

FOR THE MOUSSE

500g/1lb 2oz mixed berries
icing sugar, to taste, plus extra for
    dusting
3 sheets leaf gelatine
3 egg whites
140g/5oz golden caster sugar
300ml/½ pint double cream, whipped

1 Heat oven to 180C/160C fan/gas 4. Beat the butter with the sugar. Beat in the flour, baking powder, vanilla and eggs. Pour the batter into a lined 24cm-round loose-bottomed cake tin. Bake for 30 minutes.
2 Remove the cake from the tin; cool on a wire rack, leaving the base paper on the bottom of the cake. When the cake is cool, cut it in half horizontally. Line the tin with cling film. Put the top of the cake in the tin.
3 To make the mousse, put the berries in a pan over a low heat and bring to a simmer. Sweeten to taste with icing sugar. Pop into a blender and purée, then sieve. Soak the gelatine in water until floppy, stir into the hot berry purée. Set aside to cool.
4 Whisk the egg whites to peaks, then whisk in the caster sugar in four batches until you have a stiff, glossy meringue. Fold in the berry purée, then the cream. Pour on to the cake base. Lay the other piece of sponge on top, paper-side up. Freeze until 1 hour before needed, then peel off the paper. Dust with icing sugar.

PER SERVING 333 kcals, protein 5g, carbs 32g, fat 22g, sat fat 12g, fibre 1g, sugar 26g, salt 0.4g

Decadent chocolate truffle torte

The best thing about this mouthwatering chocolate truffle torte is there's no cooking necessary. Serve in thin slices as it is very rich.

TAKES 1 HOUR • SERVES 12
250g/9oz dark chocolate
2 tbsp golden syrup
600ml carton double cream
4 tsp instant coffee granules
1 tsp ground cinnamon
cocoa powder, for dusting
chopped hazelnuts, to decorate

1 Put the chocolate, syrup and a quarter of the cream into a large heatproof bowl. Stand the bowl over (not in) a pan of hot water on a low heat until melted, about 15-20 minutes. Remove and stir, then leave to cool a little.

2 Take a plastic folder and cut it along the bottom, then cut out a disc to fit in the bottom of a 23cm loose bottomed tin and 3 strips to line the sides. Pour the rest of the cream, coffee and cinnamon into a large bowl, whisk until thick, then gently fold in the cooled chocolate until evenly mixed. Pour into the tin.

3 Chill in the fridge until firm, at least an hour or overnight. Remove from the tin and invert a serving plate over the torte and turn upside down. Peel away the plastic. Dust all over with cocoa and scatter with nuts.

PER SERVING 331 kcals, protein 2g, carbs 17g, fat 29g, sat fat 18g, fibre 1g, sugar 15g, salt 0.09g

Raspberry Martini fizz

Impress your guests with this stylish cocktail – delicious berries with gin, prosecco and vermouth.

TAKES 10 MINUTES ● MAKES 8 (WITH ENOUGH FOR A TOP-UP)

350ml/12fl oz Martini Rosso
150ml/¼ pint gin
4 tsp icing sugar
24 frozen raspberries
2 bottles chilled prosecco or other sparkling wine

1 Mix the Martini and gin together, and chill, or store in a bottle if making ahead. If you have room in your fridge or freezer, chill the eight champagne glasses too.

2 When your guests are due to arrive, spoon ½ teaspoon of the icing sugar into each of the eight champagne glasses. Pour over the Martini mixture, mix with a spoon and add three frozen raspberries to each. Top up with the sparkling wine just before serving.

PER COCKTAIL 242 kcals, protein 1g, carbs 14g, fat none, sat fat none, fibre none, sugar 14g, salt none

Creamy pesto with prosciutto dippers

Barely any more effort than opening a bag of crisps – and your guests will be so much more impressed with this!

TAKES 15 MINUTES ● **SERVES 8**
300g tub light soft cheese
2 tbsp basil pesto
140g pack grissini (bread sticks)
90g pack prosciutto
1 tbsp pine nuts
extra virgin olive oil, for drizzling

1 Mix the cheese with the pesto.
2 Halve each breadstick and cut the prosciutto into strips and wrap one around the end of each grissini.
3 Scatter the pine nuts over the dip and drizzle with extra virgin olive oil before serving with the prosciutto dippers alongside.

PER SERVING 179 kcals, protein 9g, carbs 14g, fat 10g, sat fat 4g, fibre 1g, sugar 3g, salt 1.22g

Easy mezze

Good quality ready-prepared items from the supermarket make this the easiest-ever starter.

TAKES 15 MINUTES ● SERVES 6

6 flatbreads or 9 pitta breads
tub of houmous
1 tbsp toasted sesame seeds
little olive oil
2–3 heads chicory
tub olives
any Middle Eastern or Turkish-style
   nibbles you like

FOR THE FETA DIP

200g pack feta
200g/7oz Greek yogurt
few dill leaves

1 To make the dip, whizz the feta and yogurt in a food processor until smooth, then scrape into a serving bowl and chill.
2 To serve, warm the flatbreads or pittas and cook any nibbles, according to the pack instructions. Scrape the houmous into a serving dish, scatter with the seeds and drizzle with oil. Scatter the feta dip with chopped dill and a little black pepper. Separate the chicory leaves into a bowl and serve everything in the middle of the table.

PER SERVING 606 kcals, protein 20g, carbs 58g, fat 35g, sat fat 10g, fibre 6g, sugar 6g, salt 4.16g

Spiced swede fritters

The mild flavour of swede is a great vehicle for vibrant spices, so this twist on Indian vegetable pakoras really works.

TAKES 55 MINUTES • SERVES 4

1 swede (about 650g/1lb 7oz), peeled
   and diced into small chunks
75g/2½oz plain flour
100ml/3½fl oz créme fraîche
1 egg, beaten
1 red chilli, deseeded and finely
   chopped
1 red onion, finely chopped
1 tsp cayenne pepper
2 tsp garam masala
½ tsp ground turmeric
1 tsp crushed coriander seeds
small handful coriander, chopped
sunflower oil, for frying
mango chutney, to serve

1 Cook the swede in a pan of boiling water for 15 minutes until tender, then drain well.

2 In a large bowl, mix together the flour, créme fraîche and egg to make a smooth, thick batter. Stir in the chilli, onion, spices and chopped coriander, then season generously. Very roughly mash the swede and stir into the mixture.

3 Heat a splash of the oil in a large non-stick pan and cook small, flattened spoonfuls of the mixture for 2 minutes on each side until crisp and browned. Serve hot with chutney.

PER SERVING 242 kcals, protein 6g, carbs 23g, fat 14g, sat fat 7g, fibre 3g, sugar 9g, salt 0.1g

Smoked mackerel & horseradish cups

Quick and impressive, this no-cook mackerel pâté starter won't keep you in the kitchen for long.

TAKES 20 MINUTES, PLUS CHILLING
- **SERVES 6**

100g/4oz cottage cheese
1 tbsp creamed horseradish
50ml/2fl oz soured cream
3 smoked mackerel fillets
small handful chives, snipped
juice ½ lemon, plus lemon halves
    to squeeze over
12 large white or red chicory leaves

1 Mix together the cottage cheese, horseradish and soured cream, and leave to sit for 10 minutes.

2 Remove the skin and any bones from the mackerel, break into thumb-sized pieces and pop into a food processor. Pulse briefly to break up the chunks; it shouldn't be too fine. Turn out into a large bowl.

3 Mix the chives into the mackerel evenly, then fold in the cream mixture and lemon juice. Chill in the fridge for 20 minutes.

4 To serve, spoon some mackerel mix into each chicory leaf. Arrange on a large plate with lemon halves for squeezing over and serve with some drinks.

PER SERVING 153 kcals, protein 8g, carbs 1g, fat 13g, sat fat 4g, fibre none, sugar 1g, salt 1.11g

Chargrilled vegetable salad

For a real Mediterranean starter or light supper, serve these chargrilled vegetables with torn buffalo mozzarella.

TAKES 1 HOUR 20 MINUTES

● **SERVES 6**

2 red peppers
3 tbsp olive oil, plus extra for drizzling (optional)
1 tbsp red wine vinegar
1 small garlic clove, crushed
1 red chilli, deseeded and finely chopped
1 aubergine, cut into 1cm/½in rounds
1 large courgette, cut into 1cm rounds
2 red onions, sliced about 1.5cm/⅔in thick but kept as whole slices
6 plump sun-dried tomatoes in oil, drained and torn into strips
handful black olives
large handful basil, roughly torn
2 × 125g torn buffalo mozzarella balls or crumbled feta, to serve (optional)

1 First, blacken the peppers all over – do this directly over a flame, over hot coals or under a hot grill. When completely blackened, put them in a bowl, cover with a plate and leave to cool.

2 While the peppers are cooling, mix the oil, vinegar, garlic and chilli marinade in a bowl. On a hot barbecue or griddle pan, chargrill the aubergine, courgette and onions until they have defined grill marks on both sides and are starting to soften. The cooking time will depend on the intensity of your grill. Put the cooked vegetables straight into the marinade, breaking the onions up into rings.

3 When the peppers are cool enough to handle, peel, remove the stalk and scrape out the seeds. Cut into strips and toss through the veg with any juice from the bowl. Mix in the tomatoes, olives, basil and seasoning. Drizzle with more oil, if you like, and serve either on its own or with mozzarella or feta.

PER SERVING 126 kcals, protein 3g, carbs 10g, fat 9g, sat fat 1g, fibre 4g, sugar 7g, salt 0.66g

Herbed lamb cutlets with roasted vegetables

This traybake is so tasty and served with some toasted pitta bread and a big Greek salad it makes an impressive looking yet casual dinner party main course.

TAKES 1 HOUR • SERVES 4

2 peppers, any colour, deseeded and
    cut into chunky pieces
1 large sweet potato, peeled and cut
    into chunky pieces
2 courgettes, sliced into chunks
1 red onion, cut into wedges
1 tbsp olive oil
8 lean lamb cutlets
1 tbsp thyme leaves, chopped
2 tbsp mint leaves, chopped
Greek salad and toasted pitta bread,
    to serve

1 Heat oven to 220C/200C fan/gas 7. Put the peppers, sweet potato, courgettes and onion on a large baking tray and drizzle over the oil. Season with lots of ground black pepper. Roast for 25 minutes.

2 Meanwhile, trim the lamb of as much fat as possible. Mix the herbs with a few twists of ground black pepper and pat all over the lamb.

3 Take the vegetables out of the oven, turn over and push to one side of the tray. Place the cutlets on the hot tray and return to the oven for 10 minutes.

4 Turn the cutlets and cook for a further 10 minutes or until the vegetables and lamb are tender and lightly charred. Mix everything on the tray and serve with Greek salad and toasted pitta bread.

PER SERVING 429 kcals, protein 19g, carbs 23g, fat 29g, sat fat 13g, fibre 6g, sugar 12g, salt 0.2g

Steak with mushroom puff tartlets

These are sort of deconstructed Beef Wellingtons, but the result is much lighter.

TAKES 55 MINUTES • **SERVES 2**

100g/4oz ready-made puff pastry

1 tbsp olive oil, plus a little extra for griddling

1 shallot, finely chopped

100g/4oz chestnut mushrooms, chopped

1 tsp chopped thyme, plus sprigs to garnish

3 tbsp port or Madeira

1 tbsp double cream

2 fillet steaks (about 140g/5oz each)

1 Heat oven to 200C/180C fan/gas 6. Roll out the pastry to about the thickness of a £1 coin. Cut out two 12cm/4½in circles. Score a circle 2cm/¾in from the edge. Prick the pastry inside the border and lift onto a baking sheet. Bake for 20–25 minutes. Press the risen middles down.

2 Heat the oil in a pan, add the shallot, then fry until softened. Add the mushrooms and thyme, then fry until the mushrooms are softened and any liquid has almost gone. Add the port or Madeira, then bubble for 2 minutes. Add the cream, simmer for 1 minute more until the sauce is slightly thickened. Set aside.

3 Rub the steaks with a little oil and some seasoning. Heat a griddle pan until hot. Cook the steaks for 2–3 minutes on each side for medium–rare, a bit more if you like your steaks well done. Cover the steaks with foil; rest them for 5 minutes.

4 Warm the mushroom mixture over a low heat. Set the tartlets on warm plates and spoon over the mushroom mixture. Sit the steaks on top with a sprig of thyme.

PER SERVING 565 kcals, protein 42g, carbs 22g, fat 34g, sat fat 12g, fibre 1g, sugar 4g, salt 0.61g

Moroccan meatball tagine with lemon & olives

A wonderfully aromatic North African lamb casserole with a citrus tang – great with fluffy couscous or fresh crusty bread.

TAKES 1 HOUR 5 MINUTES • **SERVES 4**

3 onions, peeled
500g/1lb 2oz minced lamb
zest and juice 1 unwaxed lemon, plus
    1 whole unwaxed lemon, quartered
1 tsp ground cumin
1 tsp ground cinnamon
pinch cayenne pepper
small bunch flat-leaf parsley, chopped
2 tbsp olive oil
thumb-sized piece ginger, peeled and
    grated
1 red chilli, deseeded and finely
    chopped
pinch saffron strands
250ml/9fl oz lamb stock
1 tbsp tomato purée
100g/4oz pitted black Kalamata olives
small bunch coriander, chopped
couscous or fresh crusty bread,
    to serve

1 Put the onions in a food processor and blitz until finely chopped. Put the lamb, lemon zest, spices, parsley and half the onions in a large bowl, and season. Using your hands, mix until well combined, then shape into walnut-sized balls.

2 Heat the oil in a large flameproof dish, or tagine, with a lid, then add the remaining onions, the ginger, chilli and saffron. Cook for 5 minutes until the onion is softened and starting to colour. Add the lemon juice, stock, tomato purée and olives, then bring to the boil. Add the meatballs, one at a time, then reduce the heat, cover with the lid and cook for 20 minutes, turning the meatballs a couple of times.

3 Remove the lid, then add the coriander and lemon wedges, tucking them in among the meatballs. Cook, uncovered, for a further 10 minutes until the liquid has reduced and thickened slightly.

PER SERVING 394 kcals, protein 31g, carbs 11g, fat 26g, sat fat 9g, fibre 3g, sugar 8g, salt 1.7g

Creamy chicken with asparagus & tarragon

Although this dish looks and tastes outstanding it's so simple to make and can be on the dinner table in just 30 minutes.

TAKES 30 MINUTES • SERVES 4

500g/1lb 2oz baby new potatoes, halved
4 skinless chicken breasts
1 tbsp sunflower oil
1 large onion, chopped
2 garlic cloves, crushed
350ml/12fl oz chicken stock
small bunch tarragon
175g/6oz asparagus, trimmed
3 tbsp reduced-fat crème fraîche

1 Cook the potatoes in a large pan of boiling water for 8–10 minutes until tender, then drain and keep warm in the pan. Season the chicken with ground black pepper. Heat the oil in a large non-stick frying pan. Gently fry the chicken with the onion and garlic for 5 minutes until both are lightly browned. Turn over the chicken once and stir the onion regularly.

2 Pour over the stock, add 2 sprigs of tarragon and bring to a gentle simmer. Cook for 5 minutes, then turn the chicken, add the asparagus and cook for 3 minutes more. Chop the remaining tarragon.

3 Stir the crème fraîche and tarragon into the pan with the chicken and heat through, stirring, for a few seconds. Serve with the new potatoes.

PER SERVING 318 kcals, protein 38g, carbs 25g, fat 7g, sat fat 8g, fibre 4g, sugar 6g, salt 0.5g

Cottage pie bake

The combination of braised beef and mashed potatoes will always be a favourite.

TAKES 3½ HOURS • SERVES 6

1kg/2lb 4oz beef shin or feather blade,
   cut into very large chunks
2–4 tbsp sunflower oil
200g/7oz bacon lardons
200g/7oz shallots, peeled
2 celery sticks, chopped
3 tbsp plain flour
2 beef stock cubes
3 tbsp Worcestershire sauce
3 each thyme sprigs and bay leaves
300g/10oz baby carrots or baby
   Chantenay carrots

FOR THE MASH

1.5kg/3lb 5oz potatoes, peeled and
   cut into large chunks
25g/1oz butter
85g/3oz mature Cheddar, grated
100ml/3½fl oz milk
2 tsp English mustard powder

1 Brown the beef in the oil in a casserole or frying pan. Tip in the lardons, shallots and celery. Fry for 10 minutes. Stir in the flour until absorbed, crumble in the stock cubes, then gradually stir in 1 litre/1¾ pints water and the Worcestershire sauce. Add the herbs, the beef and any juices; cover and simmer for 1 hour. Add the carrots, cover. Simmer for another hour.
2 For the mash, boil the potatoes in salted water until tender. Drain well, return to pan over a gentle heat and allow to steam-dry for 2 minutes. Mash with the remaining ingredients, then season.
3 Heat oven to 200C/180C fan/gas 6. Strain the beef and veg into a colander set over a deep pan. Set the sauce over a high heat for 5 minutes to reduce. Shred the beef into chunky pieces and transfer to a baking dish with the veg and bacon, and some thickened sauce. Pipe or spoon on the mash. Bake for 30 minutes. The pie can be frozen for up to 3 months. If frozen, defrost thoroughly, then bake as above, but for 50 minutes–1 hour.

PER SERVING 884 kcals, protein 49g, carbs 54g, fat 53g, sat fat 21g, fibre 5g, sugar 7g, salt 2.3g

Chicken, parsnip & potato bake

This one-pot not only tastes delicious but it makes the washing up a doddle too.

TAKES 1 HOUR 10 MINUTES
- **SERVES 4**

4 chicken drumsticks or thighs (skin on)
2 red onions, cut through the root into
   6 wedges
4 small floury potatoes, cut into
   2–3cm/¾–1¼in cubes
2 parsnips, peeled and cut into
   4cm/1½in pieces
12 garlic cloves, unpeeled
100ml/3½fl oz olive oil

1 Heat oven to 220C/200C fan/gas 7. In a large bowl, mix together all the ingredients and season. Spread out in a roasting tin, season the chicken pieces with a little extra salt and pepper and put in the oven. Bake for 45 minutes– 1 hour, until the chicken is cooked through and the vegetables are golden and crispy.

PER SERVING 507 kcals, protein 28g, carbs 26g, fat 33g, sat fat 6g, fibre 5g, sugar 7g, salt 0.32g

Roast salmon with peas, potatoes & bacon

A brilliant all-in-one dish that's perfect for a Friday night fish supper with friends.

TAKES 1 HOUR 25 MINUTES
- **SERVES 4**

500g bag new potatoes, halved
2 tsp olive oil
150g pack smoked bacon lardons
whole piece skinless salmon fillet
   (about 700g/1lb 9oz)
200g/7oz frozen peas, defrosted
4 spring onions, sliced
splash white wine vinegar
small handful mint, chopped

1 Heat oven to 220C/200C fan/gas 7. Tip the potatoes into a large shallow roasting tin and toss with 1 teaspoon of the olive oil and some seasoning. Roast for 20 minutes until just starting to colour, then scatter over the lardons and return to the oven for 10 minutes to crisp up.

2 Remove the tin from the oven, push the potatoes and bacon to the sides and lay the salmon in the middle. Brush with the remaining oil, season, then return to the oven and cook for 20 minutes more until the salmon is just cooked through. Meanwhile, cook the peas in boiling water for 2 minutes and drain.

3 When the fish is cooked, lift it to a serving dish. Stir the peas and spring onions through the potatoes, drizzle with a splash of vinegar, stir through the mint and season to taste. Spoon around the salmon and serve.

PER SERVING 548 kcals, protein 48g, carbs 24g, fat 29g, sat fat 7g, fibre 4g, sugar 3g, salt 1.3g

Tandoori roast chicken

Serve this Indian-spiced bird with rice, naan bread and salad for an alternative to traditional roast chicken.

TAKES 3 HOURS, PLUS MARINATING
- **SERVES 4–6**

1.8kg/4lb chicken
2 onions, thickly sliced
1 lemon, halved
thumb-sized piece ginger, peeled and thickly sliced
400g can coconut milk
small bunch coriander, roughly chopped

FOR THE MARINADE

150g pot natural yogurt
1 tbsp tomato purée
juice 1 lemon
1 tsp each hot chilli powder, ground turmeric, ground coriander, ground cumin, garam masala and ground cinnamon
6 garlic cloves, whizzed to a paste with ½ finger-length piece ginger
few drops red food colouring (optional)

1 Mix the marinade ingredients with 2 teaspoons salt and 1 teaspoon black pepper. Slash the legs of the chicken a few times, then rub the marinade all over, including under the skin of the breast. Marinate in the fridge for up to 24 hours.

2 Heat oven to 200C/180C fan/gas 6. Put the onions, lemon halves and ginger in a roasting tin. Sit the chicken on top and roast for 1½ hours or until the thigh juices run clear when tested with a skewer.

3 When the chicken is done, lift out of the tin, sit in a new dish, cover loosely with foil and leave to rest. Fish out the ginger from the tin and discard. Scrape out the roasted middles from the lemons into a food processor, add the onions and any pan juices, and whizz to a purée. Scrape the purée back into the tin and sit on the hob. Stir in the coconut milk and bubble gently, scraping up any chicken bits that have stuck. You can add a splash of water if the sauce is too thick. Stir in the coriander and serve with the chicken.

PER SERVING (4) 482 kcals, protein 43g, carbs 12g, fat 30g, sat fat 8g, fibre 1g, sugar 9g, salt 0.7g

Cardamom meringue nests

Let your guests fill these sweetly spiced meringues at the table with one of the decadent flavoured creams.

TAKES 2 HOURS 5 MINUTES
- **SERVES 10**

6 egg whites
350g/12oz caster sugar
2 tsp cardamom powder
1 tsp cocoa

FOR THE CREAMS

2 × 300ml tubs extra thick double cream
50g/2oz icing sugar
50g/2oz chopped pistachios
4 passion fruit, flesh scraped out from shells

1 Heat oven to 150C/130C fan/gas 2 and line 2 baking sheets with parchment. Put the egg whites in a clean bowl and beat with an electric whisk to stiff peaks. Whisk in the sugar, 1 tablespoon at a time, until thickened and glossy. Fold in the cardamom.

2 Using a metal spoon, dollop small spoonfuls, evenly spaced, onto the baking sheets, to make around 48 mini meringues. With the back of the spoon, lightly hollow out the centres. Dust with cocoa and bake for 1 hour until crisp. Turn off the oven and leave in the oven to cool.

3 Meanwhile make the cream. Beat the double cream and icing sugar until combined, divide into two bowls. Fold through some of the nuts into one, then scrape into a serving dish and scatter with the rest of the nuts. Ripple most of the passion fruit through the other, put into a serving dish then drizzle over the remaining fruit. Serve with the meringues.

PER SERVING (meringues only) 145 kcals, protein 2g, carbs 34g, fat none, sat fat none, fibre none, sugar 35g, salt 0.10g

White chocolate fondue

Divine white chocolate fondue in which to dip summer fruits, and if you're feeling really indulgent try dipping in marshmallows and biscotti too.

TAKES 10 MINUTES ● SERVES 4

200g/7oz coarsely chopped, good-quality white chocolate
50g/2oz unsalted butter
150ml double cream
1 tsp vanilla extract
500g/1lb 2oz chilled cherries, blackberries or strawberries, or a mixture of all three

1 Combine the chocolate, butter, cream and vanilla extract in a heatproof bowl set over a pan of simmering water. Heat until melted and smooth, stirring occasionally – about 5 minutes.
2 Transfer to a fondue pot or warm serving bowl and serve with the chilled cherries or berries.

PER SERVING 577 kcals, protein 6g, carbs 40g, fat 45g, sat fat 26g, fibre 1g, sugar 24g, salt 0.17g

Pimm's iced tea

Mixing this summer favourite with ice-cold mint & citrus tea makes a less sweet but every bit as refreshing alternative to the traditional English drink.

TAKES 20 MINUTES • SERVES 6

4 tea bags
20g pack mint
100g/4oz caster sugar
juice 2 large oranges, plus slices to garnish
juice 2 lemons, plus slices to garnish
400ml/14fl oz Pimm's No 1
a few sliced strawberries, to garnish
plenty of ice, to serve

1 Put the tea bags and half the mint into a large jug, then pour over 1.2litres/2 pints boiling water from the kettle. Leave to infuse for 10 minutes, then remove the bags and stir in the sugar.
2 Once cool, remove the mint, add the orange juice, lemon juice and Pimm's, and chill thoroughly. Can be made up to a day ahead. Serve over plenty of ice garnished with slices of orange, lemon and strawberry, and the remaining mint sprigs.

PER SERVING 146 kcals, protein 1g, carbs 17g, fat none, sat fat none, fibre none, sugar 17g, salt 0.04g

Roasted butternut squash soup

For a change from bread make little tarts to accompany this soup – simply cut circles from a puff pastry sheet, top with sliced goat's cheese and bake until golden.

TAKES 50 MINUTES ● SERVES 4

70g pack cubetti di pancetta
1 butternut squash, peeled and
   chopped
1 large onion, chopped
2 garlic cloves, chopped
1 tbsp clear honey
3 rosemary sprigs
600ml/1 pint chicken stock
150ml/¼ pint white wine
100ml/3½fl oz double cream
juice 1 lemon
25g/1oz toasted pine nuts, to garnish

1 Heat oven to 220C/200C fan/gas 7. Put the pancetta in a frying pan and fry until crispy. Set aside. Put the squash, onion and garlic in a large roasting tin. Add the honey and rosemary, then roast for about 25 minutes, turning the squash halfway through, until cooked, tender and golden brown.

2 Remove the tin from the oven, take out the rosemary and discard. Transfer the contents of the tin to a food processor with the stock, wine, cream and lemon juice. Season, then blend until smooth.

3 Transfer the mixture to a large pan and reheat. Divide the soup among individual bowls and top each with a sprinkle of pine nuts and the pancetta.

PER SERVING 342 kcals, protein 12g, carbs 24g, fat 21g, sat fat 9g, fibre 5g, sugar 15g, salt 0.83

Parsnip soup with parsley cream

Making a topping for a soup is a great way of adding texture and giving a more dinner-party feel.

TAKES 1 HOUR 25 MINUTES

- **SERVES 6**

1 tbsp olive oil
1 onion, finely chopped
700g/1lb 9oz parsnips, cut into chunks
3 bay leaves
400ml/14fl oz milk
400ml/14fl oz vegetable stock

FOR THE PARSLEY CREAM

2 × 80g packs curly parsley
150ml/¼ pint double cream
150ml/¼ pint whipping cream, whipped to soft peaks

FOR THE GARNISH

1 parsnip, cut into small cubes
1 tbsp olive oil

1 Heat the oil in a pan and fry the onion until soft. Stir in the parsnips, bay leaves, milk and stock, bring to the boil and simmer gently until the parsnip is very soft. Remove the bay leaves and strain, but reserve, the liquid. Whizz the parsnips in a blender, slowly add enough liquid until you reach a lovely soup consistency.

2 For the parsley purée, blanch the parsley in boiling salted water for 30 seconds, then refresh in ice water – this keeps the green colour, drain. Bring the double cream to the boil. Whizz the parsley, slowly adding hot cream until smooth. Cool. Fold the purée through the whipped cream until nice and green. Season and chill.

3 Heat the olive oil in a pan, and fry the parsnip cubes until golden. Keep warm. To serve, reheat the soup, season, then ladle into bowls. Add a spoonful of the parsley cream and some fried parsnips.

PER SERVING 393 kcals, protein 7g, carbs 25g, fat 30g, sat fat 15g, fibre 8g, sugar 15g, salt 0.32g

Double-baked Cheddar soufflés

Double-baked soufflés are great for entertaining as you can cook them several hours in advance then re-bake just before serving.

TAKES 1 HOUR 25 MINUTES
- **MAKES 8**

425ml/¾ pint milk
1 small onion, thickly sliced
pinch ground nutmeg
2 fresh or dried bay leaves
4 tbsp butter, plus extra for greasing
7 tbsp plain flour
1 heaped tsp English mustard
4 eggs, separated
140g/5oz extra mature Cheddar
   cheese, finely grated
150ml pot double cream

1 Heat oven to 180C/160C fan/gas 4. Put the milk, onion, nutmeg and bay leaves into a pan. Bring to the boil, then strain. Butter 8 × 150ml ramekins and arrange them in a roasting tin.

2 Melt the butter. Stir in the flour and cook for 1 minute, stirring. Take off the heat and gradually whisk in the milk until smooth. Return to the hob and stir until the sauce boils and thickens, tip into a bowl and mix in the mustard, yolks and three-quarters of the cheese. In another big bowl, whisk the egg whites until stiff.

3 Carefully fold the whites into the cheese mix and fill ramekins two thirds full. Pour in boiling water to reach halfway up the ramekins. Bake for 15-20 minutes or until risen and just set. Take out of the tin, cool.

4 Heat oven to 220C/200C fan/gas 7. Loosen the soufflés around the edges, then turn out into a shallow ovenproof dish. Sprinkle on cheese, add cream then bake for 10-12 minutes until puffed and golden. Serve immediately.

PER SOUFFLÉ 336 kcals, protein 12g, carbs 14g, fat 26g, sat fat 15g, fibre 1g, sugar 4g, salt 0.63g

Crab cakes with dill mayonnaise

Perfect canapés for nibbling at drinks parties or as a smart starter too.

TAKES 45 MINUTES, PLUS CHILLING
- **SERVES 4**

250g/9oz potatoes, diced
300g/10oz white crabmeat
1 tbsp capers, rinsed, drained and
　finely chopped
2 spring onions, finely chopped
zest and juice 1 lemon, plus extra
　wedges to serve
small bunch dill, finely chopped
4 tbsp good-quality mayonnaise
2 tbsp plain flour
1 egg, lightly beaten
85g/3oz dried breadcrumbs
sunflower oil, for shallow frying

1 Boil the potatoes in a pan of salted water for about 15 minutes, drain, then return to the pan. Leave to steam dry for 5 minutes. Mash, then leave to cool.

2 In a bowl, mix the crabmeat, capers, spring onions, lemon zest and half the juice with half the dill. Stir in the mashed potato, add seasoning, then shape the mixture into 12 round patties. Transfer these to the fridge for 20 minutes.

3 To make the dill mayonnaise, mix the mayo with the remaining lemon juice and dill. Put this in the fridge for later.

4 Put the flour, egg and breadcrumbs on three separate plates. Dust the crab cakes all over with flour, then dip into the egg and finally coat with breadcrumbs, chill for 15 minutes or overnight.

5 Add enough sunflower oil to a frying pan to come about 1cm/½in up the side. Heat the oil, then slide the crab cakes in. Cook for about 3 minutes each side until crisp and golden. Keep warm – or serve right away with mayonnaise and lemon wedges.

PER SERVING 448 kcals, protein 21g, carbs 33g, fat 27g, sat fat 4g, fibre 2g, sugar 2g, salt 1.65g

Irish stew

The trick with this classic one-pot is to use a cheaper cut of meat, which means you'll skimp on price but not quality.

TAKES 2½ HOURS • SERVES 6

1 tbsp sunflower oil
200g/7oz smoked streaky bacon, preferably in one piece, fat removed and cut into chunks
900g/2lb stewing lamb, cut into large chunks
5 medium onions, sliced
5 carrots, sliced into chunks
3 bay leaves
small bunch thyme
100g/4oz pearl barley
850ml/1½ pints lamb stock
6 medium potatoes, cut into chunks
small knob of butter
3 spring onions, finely sliced

1 Heat oven to 160C/140C fan/gas 3. Heat the oil in a large flameproof casserole. Sizzle the bacon for 4 minutes until crisp. Turn up the heat, then cook the lamb for 6 minutes until brown. Remove the meats with a slotted spoon. Add the onions, carrots and herbs to the pan, then cook for about 5 minutes until softened. Return the meat to the pan, stir in the pearl barley, pour over the stock, then bring to a simmer.

2 Sit the chunks of potato on top of the stew, cover, then braise in the oven, undisturbed, for about 1½ hours until the potatoes are soft and the meat is tender. The stew can now be chilled and kept in the fridge for 2 days, then reheated in a low oven or on top of the stove.

3 To serve, when heated through, remove from the oven, dot the potatoes with butter, scatter with the spring onions and serve scooped straight from the dish.

PER SERVING 627 kcals, protein 49g, carbs 44g, fat 30g, sat fat 14g, fibre none, sugar 11g, salt 2.13g

Thai beef curry

You can use a shop-bought paste for this curry, but it's really worth making the effort to prepare this authentic Thai one.

TAKES 5 HOURS ● SERVES 6–8

2–3 tbsp groundnut oil

2kg/4lb 8oz beef short ribs (bone-in, ribs left whole) or brisket, cut into large chunks

large bunch coriander

2 lemongrass stalks, 1 roughly chopped, 1 bashed

3 garlic cloves, chopped

1–2 chillies, roughly chopped and deseeded (optional)

2cm/¾in-piece galangal or ginger, peeled and chopped

50ml/2fl oz rice wine vinegar

50ml/2fl oz fish sauce, plus extra to taste (optional)

2 tbsp palm or light brown soft sugar, plus extra to taste (optional)

400g can coconut milk

2 star anise

6 kaffir lime leaves

juice 2 limes, plus wedges to serve

1 Heat oven to 200C/180C fan/gas 6. Heat a little of the oil in a large ovenproof pan with a lid and brown the beef in batches. Remove the browned meat to a plate, reserving any juices.

2 Meanwhile, in a mini chopper or food processor, whizz half the coriander, the chopped lemongrass, the garlic, chillies and galangal or ginger with the rest of the oil until you have a rough paste.

3 Heat the paste in the lidded pan for a few minutes, then add the beef and all the remaining ingredients, apart from the remaining coriander and the lime wedges and juice. Bring to the boil then pop the lid on and transfer to the oven for 4–4½ hours, or until the meat is falling off the bone.

4 If using beef ribs, remove the bones then shred the meat with two forks. If the sauce is too thin, strain it off and boil it to reduce. Stir in the remaining coriander and the lime juice, then season with more fish sauce or sugar, if you like.

PER SERVING (6) 520 kcals, protein 33g, carbs 6g, fat 40g, sat fat 20g, fibre none, sugar 3g, salt 0.2g

Slow-roasted tomato & Gruyère tart

Slow-roasting tomatoes intensifies their flavour and sweetness, and drives off some of the water that can make a tart slightly soggy.

**TAKES 1 HOUR 20–25 MINUTES,
PLUS 1½ HOURS FOR THE TOMATOES**

● **SERVES 6**

500g/1lb 2oz smallish vine tomatoes, halved
1 tbsp olive oil
handful basil leaves, torn
500g pack shortcrust pastry
plain flour, for rolling
3 tbsp pesto (choose a vegetarian one)
2 eggs
150ml pot single cream
150ml/¼pint milk
100g/4oz grated Gruyère
handful black olives

1 Heat oven to 140C/120C fan/gas 1. Start with the filling. Arrange the tomatoes over a baking sheet, cut-sides up. Brush lightly with oil and put a little basil on top of each. Bake for 1½ hours until the tomatoes are semi-dried. Remove from the oven and increase the heat to 190C/170C fan/gas 5.

2 Roll out the pastry on a floured surface. Line a 25cm/10in flan tin; no need to trim off the excess at this stage. Line the pastry with greaseproof paper and fill with baking beans. Bake for 15 minutes, then remove the paper and beans, and cook until crisp and golden. Using a small, sharp knife, carefully trim off excess pastry.

3 Spread the pesto over the base of the case. Whisk the eggs, then whisk in the cream and milk. Season, then stir in the cheese. Pour into the pastry case and arrange the tomatoes over the top, cut-sides up. Scatter with olives and bake for 25-30 minutes until puffed and golden, cool slightly before serving.

PER SERVING 496 kcals, protein 17g, carbs 30g, fat 35g, sat fat 18g, fibre 2g, sugar 5g, salt 1g

Crispy Greek-style pie

Got friends coming round unexpectedly? This rather fancy-looking pie takes just ten minutes to get ready for the oven, so it's perfect for last-minute entertaining.

SERVES 4 • TAKES 40 MINUTES
200g/7oz bag spinach leaves
175g/6oz jar sundried tomatoes in oil, oil drained and reserved and tomatoes chopped
100g/4oz vegetarian feta, crumbled
2 eggs
½ × 250g pack filo pastry

1 Put the spinach into a large pan. Pour over a couple of tablespoons water, then cook until just wilted. Remove and once cool squeeze out any water and roughly chop. Put into a bowl with the tomatoes, feta and eggs. Season and mix well.

2 Take a sheet of pastry at a time, keeping the rest covered to stop it drying out, and brush with some of the sundried tomato oil. Drape oil-side down in a 22cm/9in loose-bottomed cake tin so that some of the pastry hangs over the side. Brush oil on another piece of pastry and place in the tin, just a little further round. Keep placing the pastry pieces in the tin until you have roughly three layers, then spoon over the filling. Pull the sides into the middle, scrunch up and make sure the filling is covered. Brush with a little more oil.

3 Heat oven to 180C/160C fan/gas 4. Cook the pie for 30 minutes until the pastry is crisp and golden brown. Remove from the cake tin, slice into wedges and serve with salad.

PER SERVING 260 kcals, protein 13g, carbs 23g, fat 14g, sat fat 5g, fibre 3g, sugar 5g, salt 3g

Chicken, bacon & potato stew

Full of delicious simple flavours, even the trickiest of eaters will love this warming stew.

TAKES 2½ HOURS • SERVES 6

1 tbsp olive oil

8 bone-in chicken thighs, skin removed

2 tbsp plain flour, seasoned with salt and pepper

12 rashers smoked streaky bacon, chopped

200g/7oz shallots, peeled

350g/12oz baby new potatoes, larger ones halved

few thyme sprigs

200ml/7fl oz white wine

500ml/18fl oz hot chicken stock

280ml pot buttermilk

squeeze lemon juice

2 tbsp tarragon, chopped

crusty bread and green salad, to serve

1 Heat oven to 180C/fan 160C/gas 4. Heat the oil in a large flameproof pan with a lid. Dust the chicken in the seasoned flour then brown the meat for about 10 minutes, until it has a nice golden colour, then remove and set aside. Tip in the bacon and shallots, and brown these too.

2 Tip in the remaining ingredients except the buttermilk, lemon juice and 1 of the tablespoons of tarragon, bring to the boil, then cover and cook in the oven for 1 hour. Remove the pan from the oven, stir in the buttermilk, then return to the oven and cook for 30 minutes more, uncovered.

3 Stir in the lemon juice and remaining tarragon, season, then serve with crusty bread and a crunchy green salad.

PER SERVING 284 kcals, protein 2g, carbs 12g, fat 13g, sat fat 4g, fibre 2g, sugar 4g, salt 1.7g

Mexican beef chilli

Greet your guests as they come in from the cold with a delicious bowl of spicy braised beef. The amount of chilli paste we have used is suitable for a medium heat.

TAKES 2¾ HOURS
- **SERVES 15, EASILY HALVED**

up to 6 tbsp sunflower oil
4kg/9lb stewing beef
4 white onions, sliced
4 tbsp chipotle chilli paste
8 garlic cloves, crushed
50g/2oz ginger, grated
1 tbsp ground cumin
2 tsp ground cinnamon
1 tbsp plain flour
2 litres/3½ pints beef stock
3 × 400g cans chopped tomatoes
1 tbsp dried oregano
5 × 400g cans pinto or kidney beans, rinsed and drained
garlic bread and tomato and avocado salad, to serve

1 Heat a small drizzle of the oil in an extra-large flameproof dish. Brown the meat in batches, adding a drop more oil if needed, remove from the dish and set aside. Add 1 tablespoon of the oil to the dish, then the onions, and cook for 7–10 minutes until caramelised.

2 Stir in the chipotle paste, garlic, ginger, cumin, cinnamon and flour to the pan and cook for 2 minutes. Gradually add the stock, stirring all the time, so it's fully mixed in with the other ingredients. Add the tomatoes and oregano, season and simmer for 10 minutes.

3 Now tip in the beef, cover and simmer very gently for about 1¾ hours until tender, removing the lid and adding the beans for the final 15 minutes. If the sauce is thin, let it boil down for a further 5–10 minutes with the lid off. Before serving, adjust the seasoning. Serve with garlic bread and a tomato and avocado salad.

PER SERVING 551 kcals, protein 69g, carbs 19g, fat 22g, sat fat 8g, fibre 7g, sugar 6g, salt 1.7g

Cardamom lamb hotpot

*This freezes really well, just cool completely then wrap and freeze. Thaw in the fridge
then cook as below adding an extra 30 minutes to the cooking time.*

TAKES 4¼ HOURS • SERVES 8

2 large onions, roughly chopped
6 garlic cloves
50g/2oz root ginger, roughly chopped
3 tbsp sunflower oil
30 cardamom pods, seeds removed
    and ground
2 tsp ground coriander
1kg/2lb 4oz lean diced lamb
700ml/1¼ pints lamb stock
2 fresh red chillies, deseeded and
    chopped
3 tbsp tomato purée
100g/4oz creamed coconut (from a
    block), chopped
20 curry leaves
2 aubergines, cubed
400g bag spinach

FOR THE POTATO TOPPING

1.5kg/3lb 5oz large new potatoes,
    unpeeled
2 tbsp sunflower oil
3 tbsp tamarind paste
1 tsp each turmeric and cumin seeds
10 curry leaves

1 Put the onion, garlic and ginger in a food processor and blend to a purée. Heat the oil in a large pan and fry the onion purée for 20 minutes until starting to colour, stirring often. Add the cardamom and coriander with the lamb and cook until brown, pour in the stock, chilli, purée, coconut and curry leaves, then cover and simmer for 1½ hours, adding the aubergines after an hour.

2 Meanwhile, make the topping. Boil the potatoes whole for 15-20 mins until just tender, then drain and cool. Wilt the spinach in a colander with a kettle of water, cool and squeeze to remove the water. Peel and thickly slice the potatoes, then toss with the oil, tamarind, turmeric, cumin seeds, curry leaves and seasoning.

3 Heat the oven to 160C/180C fan/gas 4. Stir the spinach into the curry and spoon into a large ovenproof dish. Pile the potatoes on top and lightly press down. Bake for 1hourr 20 minutes, until golden.

PER SERVING 578 kcals, protein 38g, carbs 43g, fat 28g, sat fat 13g, fibre 7g, sugar 14g, salt 0.5g

Italian vegetable bake

A delicious one-pot with all the classic flavours most loved in Italian cooking.

TAKES 1½ HOURS • SERVES 6

4 garlic cloves, 3 crushed, 1 left whole
400g can chopped tomatoes
bunch oregano, leaves chopped
large pinch dried chilli flakes
about 300g/10oz baby or normal
    aubergines, sliced
2 courgettes, sliced
½ × large jar roasted red peppers
3 beef tomatoes, sliced
bunch basil, torn (save a few leaves for
    sprinkling over)
small baguette, sliced and toasted
2 × 125g balls mozzarella, torn
green salad, to serve

1 Put the crushed garlic, canned tomatoes, half the oregano leaves, chilli and some seasoning in a pan, and simmer while you chop the rest of the vegetables.
2 Heat oven to 200C/180C fan/gas 6. Tip a little of the sauce into an ovenproof dish and then layer up half the aubergines, courgettes, red peppers, tomatoes, basil and the remaining oregano. Top with half the bread, rubbed with the whole garlic clove, half the mozzarella and half the rest of the tomato sauce. Repeat with the remaining ingredients, finishing with the sliced bread and mozzarella. Bake for 50 minutes, covering with foil if it gets too golden. Serve with a green salad.

PER SERVING 274 kcals, protein 14g, carbs 31g, fat 10g, sat fat 6g, fibre 4g, sugar 8g, salt 0.9g

Brownie fudge pie

This gooey chocolate dessert is given a hint of spice with cinnamon in the pastry. It freezes really well so is a great make ahead dessert.

TAKES 1½ HOURS, PLUS CHILLING
● **SERVES 8**

175g/6oz plain flour, plus extra for rolling
85g/3oz butter, chopped into pieces
2 tbsp icing sugar
1 tsp ground cinnamon
3 large eggs
300g/10oz light muscovado sugar
1 tsp vanilla extract
175g/6oz butter, melted
50g/2oz plain flour
50g/2oz cocoa powder, plus extra to dust
50g/2oz macadamia nuts, chopped
50g/2oz dark chocolate, chopped
ice cream, to serve

1 Tip the flour, butter, icing sugar and cinnamon into a food processor and pulse to make crumbs. Add 2½–3 tablespoons of water and pulse until it comes together. Wrap in cling film and chill for 20 minutes.

2 Heat oven to 180C/160C fan/gas 4. Roll out the pastry on a lightly floured surface and use to line a deep 23cm-round loose-bottomed tart tin. Leave the excess pastry overhanging the edges of the tin. Line with baking parchment, fill with baking beans and chill for 15 minutes.

3 Bake for 15 minutes, remove the paper and beans, then bake for 5 minutes more.

4 Beat the eggs and sugar together to create a mousse-like texture. Stir in the vanilla and melted butter, then fold in the flour and cocoa. Scatter the nuts and chocolate over the pastry case and pour the filling on top. Bake for 30 minutes until firm with a slight wobble. Trim away the excess pastry and leave to cool.

5 Serve with a scoop of ice cream and dusting of cocoa.

PER SERVING 639 kcals, protein 7g, carbs 71g, fat 38g, sat fat 19g, fibre 2g, sugar 46g, salt 0.54g

Peanut butter cheesecake

This cheesecake is the perfect for peanut butter fans – freeze for up to 2 months and serve as a show-stopping dinner-party dessert.

TAKES 35 MINUTES, PLUS CHILLING

● **SERVES 6–8**

FOR THE BASE

oil, for greasing
50g/2oz butter
175g pack peanut cookies

FOR THE FILLING

5 leaf gelatine
500g tub ricotta
175g/6oz smooth peanut butter
175g/6oz golden syrup
150ml/¼ pint milk

TO DECORATE

300ml pot double cream
2 tbsp soft brown sugar
1 bar peanut brittle, crushed

1 Oil and line a 20cm-round loose-bottomed cake tin with cling film. Melt the butter in a pan. Crush the biscuits by bashing them in a bag with a rolling pin, then stir them into the butter until well coated. Press the mixture firmly into the base of the tin and chill.

2 Soak the gelatine in water while you make the filling. Tip the ricotta into a bowl, then beat in the peanut butter and syrup.

3 Take the soaked gelatine from the water and squeeze it dry. Put it into a pan with the milk and heat very gently until the gelatine dissolves. Beat into the peanut mixture, then tip on to the biscuit base. Chill until set. If you like you can freeze it at this point – transfer to the freezer in the tin and as soon as it is solid, cover the surface with cling film, then wrap the tin with cling film and foil.

4 To serve, if you have frozen the cheesecake, first defrost it in the fridge overnight. Whisk the cream with the sugar until it holds its shape, then spread it on top. Scatter with the peanut brittle.

PER SERVING (8) 743 kcals, protein 19g, carbs 53g, fat 52g, sat fat 22g, fibre 2g, sugar 44g, salt 0.8g

Chocolate, pistachio & nougat semifreddo

A semifreddo is the perfect solution for an effortless, frozen, creamy dessert. For this recipe, use only hard nougat or torrone – available in most good delis.

TAKES 30 MINUTES, PLUS FREEZING
● **SERVES 10**

butter, for greasing
75g/2½oz golden caster sugar
4 medium eggs
250g/9oz dark chocolate, finely
    chopped
450ml/16fl oz double cream
140g/5oz hard nougat or torrone,
    chopped into 0.5cm/¼in chunks
50g/2oz pistachio nuts, roughly
    chopped

1 Butter and line a 900g/2lb loaf tin with cling film. Bring a pan of water to a gentle simmer. Put the sugar and eggs in a heatproof bowl, then put over the simmering water – without the base touching the water – and whisk until pale, thick and doubled in volume. Remove from the heat, plunge the bottom of the bowl into cold water and continue whisking until the mixture is cool.
2 Melt the chocolate in the microwave on low, stir, then fold into the egg mixture. Whip the cream to soft peaks and fold into the chocolate and egg mixture with the chopped nougat and pistachios.
3 Pour the mixture into the loaf tin, smooth the surface with the back of a spoon, then cover and freeze until firm. This can be done up to 2 weeks ahead. To serve, turn out on to a serving dish, remove the cling film and leave in the fridge for 15 minutes to soften slightly before slicing.

PER SERVING 490 kcals, protein 6g, carbs 34g, fat 37g, sat fat 20g, fibre 1g, sugar 34g, salt 0.1g

Summer berry & lime jellies

Use whatever berries you grow in your garden and bulk them out with shop-bought if you need more.

TAKES 40 MINUTES, PLUS OVERNIGHT CHILLING • MAKES 6

450g/1lb caster sugar
zest and juice 3 limes
8 leaf gelatine
300g/10oz raspberries
300g/10oz blueberries
300g/10oz strawberries
clotted cream and shortbread,
    to serve

1 The day before serving, make the jelly by bringing 1 litre/1¾ pints water to the boil with the sugar, lime zest and juice. Meanwhile, soak the gelatine in a bowl of ice-cold water. When the sugar has dissolved, remove from the heat. Squeeze the excess water from the gelatine and add to the pan, stirring to dissolve.

2 Pass the syrup through a sieve into a bowl. Allow to cool to room temperature.

3 Ladle a layer of jelly into six ramekins or jelly moulds, scatter with a layer of raspberries. Leave in the fridge for 1 hour to set. Top up with a bit more jelly; leave to set. Continue adding jelly with a layer of strawberries then blueberries, remembering to set each layer before starting the next. Once the moulds are full, top with a bit more jelly; put in the fridge. Leave overnight to set completely.

4 To serve the jellies, briefly dip the moulds in hot water, then loosen from the sides and turn out on to plates. Serve with clotted cream and shortbread.

PER JELLY 365 kcals, protein 8g, carbs 88g, fat none, sat fat none, fibre 3g, sugar 88g, salt 0.09g

Berry shortbread cheesecake slice

A stunning centrepiece dessert that's bursting with summer flavours – perfect for a special occasion

TAKES 2 HOURS, PLUS CHILLING

● **SERVES 8**

FOR THE BASE

50g/2oz butter, melted, plus extra to grease

200g pack shortbread biscuits

FOR THE CHEESECAKE

2 × 300g tubs soft cheese

200g tub crème fraîche

1 tsp vanilla extract

175g/6oz golden caster sugar

2 tbsp plain flour

2 eggs

FOR THE TOPPING

5 tbsp seedless raspberry jam

300g/10oz mixed summer berries, such as raspberries, redcurrants, cherries and blueberries

1 Heat oven to 180C/160C fan/gas 4. Grease and line a 900g loaf tin with baking parchment. Tip the shortbread into a food processor and blitz into crumbs, or put in a plastic bag and bash with a rolling pin. Add the melted butter and mix well. Press the mix into the base of the tin.

2 Beat the soft cheese, crème fraîche, vanilla and sugar until smooth, then mix in the flour and eggs until smooth again. Pour the mix into the tin and smooth the top with a knife. Bake in the oven for 10 minutes, then lower the temperature to 120C/100C fan/gas ½ and cook for 1 hour 20 minutes or until set with a slight wobble in the centre. Turn off the heat and leave to cool in the oven. Once cool, refrigerate until chilled.

3 To make the topping, melt the jam in a small pan over a low heat with enough water to make a pouring consistency, then allow to cool completely. To serve, top the cake with the berries and drizzle with the jam.

PER SERVING 610 kcals, protein 9g, carbs 53g, fat 42g, sat fat 26g, fibre 1g, sugar 39g, salt 1.09g

Salmon & prawns with dill & lime aïoli

You can mix the aïoli ahead of time, then just keep it in the fridge until you're ready to plate up.

TAKES 15 MINUTES ● SERVES 8

400g/14oz cooked king prawns, shelled
    apart from the tail
400g/14oz smoked salmon
140g/5oz good-quality mayonnaise
2 garlic cloves, crushed
2 tbsp chopped dill, plus extra leaves
    to garnish
juice ½ lime, plus 1 cut into wedges
    to garnish
granary bread and butter, to serve
    (optional)

1 Arrange the prawns and salmon on plates.
2 Mix the mayo, garlic and chopped dill, and add lime juice to taste.
3 Put a spoonful of the aïoli on each plate, scatter over the dill leaves, add a wedge of lime and a grinding of pepper. Served with buttered granary bread, if you like.

PER SERVING 248 kcals, protein 24g, carbs 6g, fat 17g, sat fat 3g, fibre none, sugar none, salt 3.54g

Prawn bruschetta with lemony fennel salad

These also double up as delicious dinner-party canapés – make them slightly smaller and hand them around with drinks.

TAKES 15 MINUTES • SERVES 2

1 fennel bulb, thinly sliced through
   the root, green fronds reserved
1 heaped tbsp roughly chopped dill
zest and juice ½ lemon, plus wedges
   to garnish
1 tbsp olive oil
4 small slices rustic wholemeal bread,
   or 2 large cut in half
1 garlic clove, halved
140g/5oz cooked prawns
handful rocket leaves

1 Bring a pan of salted water to the boil then add the fennel slices and simmer for 2–3 minutes until just tender. Drain well and toss with the reserved fennel fronds, dill, lemon zest and juice, 2 teaspoons of the olive oil and seasoning.
2 Brush the slices of bread with the remaining oil. Put in a hot griddle pan (or under a grill) and toast on both sides until lightly charred. Rub one side of each slice with the garlic, then divide the fennel salad among them. Top with the prawns, then the rocket and serve.

PER SERVING 220 kcals, protein 21g, carbs 19g, fat 7g, sat fat 1g, fibre 5g, sugar 2g, salt 1.88g

Brie & pecan bites

These cheesy bites are a great addition when you're hosting a drinks party with canapés.

TAKES 45 MINUTES • SERVES 8

2 × 250g rounds Brie
270g pack filo pastry
50g/2oz butter, melted
2 eggs, beaten
140g/5oz pecan nuts, finely chopped
clear honey, for drizzling

1 Heat oven to 220C/200C fan/gas 7. Unwrap the cheeses and slice each in half horizontally through the centre to make four rounds. Cut each round into eight to give 32 wedges in total.

2 Unroll the pastry and take out one sheet at a time, keeping the remainder covered under a tea towel. Cut the pastry into four long strips, brush with melted butter, then place a wedge of Brie at the top of each strip. Fold the pastry over, then over again to encase the Brie, as you would a samosa, into a triangle. Dip one side of the pastry into the beaten eggs, then into the chopped pecans. Put on a baking sheet, then repeat with the remaining Brie, pastry, eggs and nuts.

3 Bake the bites for 8–10 minutes until golden. Remove from the oven and allow to stand for 2 minutes before drizzling with honey to serve.

PER SERVING 442 kcals, protein 16g, carbs 11g, fat 37g, sat fat 16g, fibre 1g, sugar 2g, salt 1g

Smoked trout salad with fennel, apple & beetroot

Delicate hot-smoked fish is perfectly complemented by crisp apple and aniseed flavours – a great start to any dinner party.

TAKES 15 MINUTES • **SERVES 2**

½ small fennel bulb, trimmed and
    thinly sliced, fronds reserved and
    chopped
1 green-skinned apple, cored,
    quartered and sliced
4 spring onions, sliced on the diagonal
100g/4oz cooked baby beetroots in
    mild vinegar, drained and quartered
140g/5oz skinless hot-smoked trout
    fillets
small bunch dill, chopped
2 tbsp low-fat natural yogurt
1 tsp horseradish sauce

1 Put the fennel in a shallow serving dish and scatter over the apple, spring onions and beetroot. Flake the trout into chunky pieces and arrange on top. Sprinkle with the fennel fronds and half the dill. Finely chop the remaining fronds and reserve.

2 Mix the yogurt and horseradish with 1 tablespoon of cold water, then stir in the reserved dill. Pour half the dressing over the salad and toss very lightly. Spoon over the remaining dressing and serve.

PER SERVING 183 kcals, protein 19g, carbs 16g, fat 5g, sat fat 1g, fibre 5g, sugar 16g, salt 1.6g

Creamy smoked salmon, leek & potato soup

Any leftovers will taste great reheated over the next couple of days.

TAKES 40 MINUTES • SERVES 8

large knob of butter
2 large leeks, halved and finely sliced
1 bay leaf
1kg/2lb 4oz floury potatoes, diced
1 litre/1¾ pints chicken or vegetable
   stock
100ml/3½fl oz double cream
200g/7oz smoked salmon, cut into
   strips
small bunch chives, snipped, to garnish

1 Heat the butter in a large pan and add the leeks and bay leaf. Cook over a low heat for 8–10 minutes or until the leek is really soft, then stir through the potatoes until coated in the butter. Pour over the stock and cream, and bring to a simmer, then gently bubble for 10–15 minutes until the potatoes are really tender.

2 Add two-thirds of the smoked salmon, stir through and season. Serve the soup in deep bowls with the remaining smoked salmon and snipped chives on the top.

PER SERVING 240 kcals, protein 14g, carbs 23g, fat 11g, sat fat 6g, fibre 3g, sugar 2g, salt 1.58g

Celeriac tartare with smoked trout

This is a twist on remoulade. Served with flaked smoked fish and dressed leaves, it makes an easy starter.

TAKES 20 MINUTES ● SERVES 4

1 small celeriac
2 × 125g packs smoked trout, flaked
100g bag rocket leaves
extra virgin olive oil, for drizzling

FOR THE TARTARE DRESSING

6 tbsp mayonnaise
small handful capers, rinsed and
    chopped
2 tbsp lemon juice
2 tbsp cornichons, finely chopped
small handful parsley leaves, finely
    chopped

1 Combine all the ingredients for the tartare dressing with some salt and set aside.
2 Peel the celeriac and either finely slice it then cut into matchsticks, or simply grate it coarsely. Mix the celeriac into the dressing until combined. Put piles of smoked trout, celeriac and rocket on to serving plates and drizzle everything with olive oil.

PER SERVING 350 kcals, protein 16g, carbs 5g, fat 30g, sat fat 5g, fibre 6g, sugar 3g, salt 2.45g

Courgette & watercress salad with grilled fish & herbed aïoli

Making aïoli takes no time the Good Food way; but if you'd rather, buy a pot of fresh mayonnaise from the chiller cabinet and add crushed garlic and herbs.

TAKES 30 MINUTES • SERVES 4

about 12 baby courgettes
3 tbsp olive oil
4 fillets sustainable white fish, skin on
juice ½ lemon
bunch mint, leaves picked
100g bag watercress (or use rocket leaves)

FOR THE HERBED AÏOLI

2 egg yolks
1 tsp Dijon mustard
1 fat garlic clove
200ml/7fl oz mild olive oil
lemon juice, to taste
handful mixed soft herbs (such as chives, parsley, mint and dill) chopped, plus extra picked leaves, to garnish

1 Heat a griddle pan. Rub the courgettes in 1 tablepoon of the oil, season, then griddle until just soft. Set aside.

2 Whizz the egg yolks for the aïoli in a processor with the mustard, garlic and plenty of salt. Gradually add the oil until thick, then season with lemon juice. It will keep for a day in the fridge.

3 Season the fish. Heat a non-stick frying pan until very hot, add 1 tablepoon of the oil, then fry the fish, skin-side down, for 3 minutes until crisp. Turn and fry the fish for just 30 seconds–1 minute more until it is cooked all the way through.

4 To serve, fold the herbs into the aïoli. Whisk 1 tablespoon oil with the lemon juice, season, then use very lightly to dress the courgettes, mint and watercress. Pile on to plates, top with fish plus a dollop of aïoli, then scatter with more herbs.

PER SERVING 605 kcals, protein 32g, carbs 2g, fat 52g, sat fat 8g, fibre 1g, sugar 2g, salt 0.37g

Potato cakes with smoked salmon

These potato cakes are traditionally made in Ireland where they're known as 'farls'. Here, we've used a classic New York bagel topping to give them a sophisticated twist.

TAKES 40 MINUTES • SERVES 4

3 medium potatoes, quartered
100g/4oz flour, plus extra for rolling and
   dusting
½ tsp baking powder

FOR THE TOPPING

150g/5oz full-fat soft cheese
200g pack smoked salmon
½ small red onion, thinly sliced
1 tbsp capers, drained
zest 1 lemon

1 Make the potato cakes. Bring a pan of salted water to the boil. Tip in the potatoes and cook until soft. Drain, then return to the hot pan for 1–2 minutes. Pass the potatoes through a sieve to get a really fine mash.

2 Weigh out 250g/9oz of the mash and put in a bowl. Tip in the flour, baking powder and 1 teaspoon salt. Mix to a soft dough. Shape into a ball and tip out onto a lightly floured surface. Roll out into a circle about 20cm/8in across and 1cm/½in thick. Cut into eight triangular wedges and dust with flour.

3 Set a large non-stick frying pan over a medium heat (no need to add oil). When hot, dry-fry the cakes for about 3–5 minutes on each side until golden and cooked through. Stir a little water into the soft cheese until it is spoonable. Put the potato cakes on plates, top with dollops of soft cheese and a smoked salmon slice, then scatter over the red onion, capers and lemon zest to finish.

PER SERVING 394 kcals, protein 18g, carbs 36g, fat 21g, sat fat 12g, fibre 2g, sugar 1g, salt 4.35g

Soy-glazed beef

Give beef a boost with this delicious soy marinade. Serve with a simple roasted red onion and new potato salad.

TAKES 1 HOUR 5 MINUTES, PLUS MARINATING ● SERVES 6

1.8kg/4lb boneless beef joint, such as sirloin or top rump

splash of brandy or bourbon (optional)

FOR THE MARINADE

4 garlic cloves, roughly chopped

1 red chilli, deseeded and roughly chopped

large knob of ginger, peeled and chopped

3 tbsp soy or teriyaki sauce

3 tbsp tomato ketchup

1 To make the marinade, blitz the garlic, chilli and ginger in a blender until finely chopped. Add the soy or teriyaki sauce and ketchup, then pulse until completely blended. Put the beef in a dish and smear over the marinade. Leave in the fridge to marinate for up to 24 hours, the longer the better.

2 To cook the beef, heat oven to 200C/180C fan/gas 6 and roast the joint for 1½ hours for medium. Baste it every so often with the sticky juices. Take the beef out, drizzle over the brandy or bourbon (if using) and flambé the meat. Leave it to rest, covered, for 15 minutes before carving.

3 Lift the meat on to a board, cover with foil and leave to rest for at least 10 minutes. Carve the beef into slices like a roast and serve with any juices drizzled on top.

PER SERVING 420 kcals, protein 62g, carbs 1g, fat 19g, sat fat 8g, fibre none, sugar 1g, salt 0.61g

Lamb tagliata with watercress & tomatoes

Traditionally, tagliata is thinly sliced beef served with rocket and shaved Parmesan,
We've given it a simple twist by using the best of the season's lamb.

TAKES 15 MINUTES, PLUS
MARINATING ● SERVES 4

handful fresh rosemary, needles
   chopped
2 tbsp extra virgin olive oil
4 thick British boneless lamb leg steaks
   or steaks cut from lamb rumps
   (about 450g/1lb in total)
250g/9oz baby plum tomatoes
1 tbsp redcurrant jelly
2 tbsp balsamic vinegar
2 tbsp capers, rinsed and drained
100g bag watercress, thick stems
   removed
100g/4oz feta, crumbled
good crusty bread, to serve

1 Rub the rosemary and 1 tablespoon of the oil over the lamb and leave to marinate for 30 minutes.
2 Heat a frying pan until very hot. Wipe most of the rosemary from the lamb, then season the steaks with plenty of flaky salt and freshly ground black pepper. Add the steaks and the tomatoes to the pan. Sear the meat for 2 minutes on one side until golden, then turn and cook for 2 minutes more. This will give pink lamb. Transfer the meat and tomatoes to a plate and leave to rest.
3 Take the pan from the heat. Spoon in the redcurrant jelly, pour in the vinegar and remaining oil, then whisk to make a warm dressing. Add the capers, plus any juices from the lamb plate.
4 Slice the lamb thickly on an angle. Spread over a large platter with the watercress and tomatoes, then finish with a crumbling of cheese. Spoon over the warm dressing and enjoy straight away with crusty bread.

PER SERVING 334 kcals, protein 28g, carbs 6g, fat 22g, sat fat 8g, fibre 2g, sugar 6g, salt 1.4g

Three-hour shoulder of lamb

Simplicity itself – cooking the shoulder slowly means the meat will melt away from the bone.

TAKES 3 HOURS 40 MINUTES
● **SERVES 4**

2 garlic cloves, finely chopped
1 tbsp oregano, roughly chopped
1 tbsp olive oil
1 shoulder of lamb, boned and tied
   (about 1.5kg/3lb 5oz)
400g/14oz pearl onions or shallots,
   peeled
250ml/9fl oz lamb stock
100g/4oz fresh peas
100g/4oz fresh broad beans
2 Little Gem lettuces, cut into quarters
juice 1 lemon
small handful mint or coriander,
   roughly chopped

1 Heat oven to 140C/120C fan/gas 1. Mix the garlic, oregano and olive oil with some salt and pepper. Slash the lamb all over and rub the mixture into the meat. Put in a deep casserole dish with the onions or shallots and pour over the stock, cover with a tight-fitting lid and cook for 3 hours.

2 Remove the lamb from the pot, stir through the peas and broad beans. Sit the lamb back on top of the vegetables and return to the oven. Increase oven temperature to 180C/160C fan/gas 4 and roast, uncovered, for another 20–30 minutes until the lamb is browned, adding the lettuce for the final 5 minutes.

3 Allow to rest for 20 minutes, then add the lemon juice and mint or coriander to the cooking juices around the lamb. Remove the string, carve into thick slices and lay them back on top of the veg to make serving easier.

PER SERVING 976 kcals, protein 72g, carbs 9g, fat 73g, sat fat 35g, fibre 5g, sugar 0.59g, salt 0.95g

Chinese braised beef with ginger

As long as you cook the beef chunks until they're melt-in-the-mouth, you can't go wrong with this dish – it has such a depth of flavour.

TAKES 3 HOURS 35 MINUTES

● **SERVES 6**

2–3 tbsp sunflower or vegetable oil

1.25kg/2lb 12oz beef shin or brisket, cut into very large chunks

2 onions

50g/2oz fresh ginger

3 garlic cloves

small bunch coriander

2 tsp Chinese five-spice

6 whole star anise

1 tsp black peppercorns

100g/4oz dark muscovado sugar

50ml/2fl oz dark soy sauce

50ml/2fl oz light soy sauce

2 tbsp tomato purée

600ml/1 pint–700ml/1¼ pints beef stock

TO SERVE

thumb-sized chunk ginger, shredded into matchsticks

1 tbsp sunflower or vegetable oil

boiled or steamed jasmine rice

1 Heat a little oil in a flameproof dish. Add the beef chunks, in batches; fry until browned. When each batch is browned, transfer to another dish. Roughly chop the onions, ginger, garlic and coriander stalks. Put in a food processor; whizz to a paste.

2 Wipe any oil out of the dish you browned the beef in. Add the paste with a splash of water; gently fry until the paste is fragrant and softened (add more water if the paste sticks). Stir in the five-spice, star anise and peppercorns, cook for 1 minute, add the sugar, soy sauces and tomato purée. Return the beef and any juices to the dish; stir in enough stock to cover. Bring to a gentle simmer. Heat oven to 160C/140C fan/gas 3. Cover the dish; put in the oven. Cook for 2½ hours.

3 Lift the beef out of the sauce and boil the sauce until reduced by about half. Meanwhile, fry the ginger in the oil until golden and crispy. Return the beef to the sauce. Serve the beef spooned over rice and scattered with the crispy ginger.

PER SERVING 405 kcals, protein 51g, carbs 26g, fat 11g, sat fat 4g, fibre 1g, sugar 23g, salt 3.96g

Venison steak with port sauce

If you're a beef-lover, give venison a go – it's rich and flavoursome, but lower in fat.

TAKES 40 MINUTES • SERVES 4

750g/1lb 10oz small potatoes, halved or quartered if some are large
2 tbsp olive oil
4 venison steaks
1 tbsp cracked black pepper
chopped parsley, to garnish (optional)
peas, to serve (optional)

FOR THE SAUCE

zest 1 orange, removed in strips, plus the juice
6 tbsp redcurrant jelly
4 tbsp port
1 cinnamon stick

1 Make the sauce by simmering all the ingredients together until the redcurrant jelly has completely melted. Keep warm.
2 Steam or simmer the potatoes until just tender, about 8 minutes, then drain well and add a few drops of the oil.
3 Lay the venison on a board. Sprinkle some of the black pepper and a little salt on each side, pressing the pepper into the steaks. Heat the remaining oil in a pan. When it has a shimmering surface, add the steaks, two at a time. Cook for two minutes on each side for rare, 3 minutes for medium and 4 minutes for well done.
4 When all the steaks are cooked, return them to the pan and pour over the sauce. Warm for 1 minute then sprinkle with parsley, if you like. Serve with the potatoes and peas, and any extra sauce spooned over.

PER SERVING 460 kcals, protein 37g, carbs 48g, fat 14g, sat fat 2g, fibre 2g, sugar 20g, salt 0.27g

Leek, goat's cheese, walnut & lemon tart

Served with a big salad and some crusty bread, this makes a filling main. Cut into six or eight and with a few mixed leaves on the side, it doubles up as a starter too.

TAKES 55 MINUTES ● SERVES 4

1 tbsp olive oil, plus extra for drizzling
   and brushing
25g/1oz butter
2 medium leeks, sliced
2 tbsp chopped thyme leaves
zest 2 lemons and juice 1 lemon
375g pack ready-rolled puff pastry
200g/7oz soft goat's cheese
50g/2oz walnut pieces
little chopped parsley, to garnish

1 Heat oven to 220C/200C fan/gas 7. Heat the olive oil in a large frying pan, then add the butter. Once sizzling, add the leeks and cook over a medium heat until softened but not coloured. Stir in the thyme and half the lemon zest, then increase the heat. Add the lemon juice and cook for about 30 seconds until the lemon juice reduces, then season well. Remove from the heat and cool slightly.

2 Unroll the pastry and lay on a baking sheet lined with baking parchment. Lightly mark a 1cm/½in border around the edges with the tip of a sharp knife, then prick the base all over with a fork.

3 Spread the lemony leeks on top of the pastry, within the border. Crumble over the cheese, scatter with the walnuts, then season with pepper. Drizzle with some olive oil, brushing the edges with a little as well.

4 Put the tart in the oven for 15–20 minutes. Scatter with parsley and the remaining lemon zest to serve.

PER SERVING 683 kcals, protein 19g, carbs 35g, fat 52g, sat fat 24g, fibre 2g, sugar 3g, salt 1.6g

Foolproof chocolate & coffee fondants

Making the ultimate show-off dessert, molten chocolate fondants, is a lot easier than you think.

TAKES 35 MINUTES • SERVES 6

175g/6oz butter, plus extra melted
 for greasing
cocoa powder, for dusting
175g/6oz good-quality dark chocolate
 (we used 70% cocoa solids)
200g/7oz golden caster sugar
4 eggs
50ml/2fl oz good-quality black coffee
 (we used espresso coffee)
85g/3oz plain flour
vanilla ice cream, to serve

1 Heat oven to 200C/180C fan/gas 6. Use a pastry brush to grease six dariole moulds or individual pudding basins really well and put in the fridge for the butter to set. Then grease again, dust with cocoa powder and set aside.

2 Melt the butter and chocolate together over a pan of barely simmering water, then remove. In a separate bowl, beat the sugar and eggs together until light and fluffy. Fold the chocolate and beaten egg together, then add the coffee and finally fold through the flour.

3 Divide the mixture among the darioles or basins. The puddings can now be frozen or chilled. Put on a baking sheet and bake for exactly 12 minutes until the mixture has puffed up and formed a crust but still has a slight wobble to it. Turn the puddings out on to serving plates and serve with a scoop of vanilla ice cream.

PER SERVING 635 kcals, protein 9g, carbs 60g, fat 42g, sat fat 23g, fibre 2g, sugar 44g, salt 0.52g

Lime possets with raspberries

You only need four ingredients for this refreshing summer dessert, plus it can be made a day ahead.

TAKES 15 MINUTES, PLUS CHILLING
- **SERVES 2**

200ml/7fl oz double cream
4 tbsp caster sugar
3 tbsp lime juice (about 3 limes), plus zest 1 lime
few raspberries, to decorate

1 Put the cream and sugar in a small pan. Heat until just boiling, then boil vigorously for 2½ minutes, while stirring constantly. Turn off the heat, stir in the lime juice and most of the zest and divide between two small pots or glasses. Chill for at least 2 hours (or overnight if you're making ahead), until set.
2 To serve, top each posset with a few raspberries and the remaining zest.

PER SERVING 619 kcals, protein 2g, carbs 34g, fat 54g, sat fat 30g, fibre none, sugar 34g, salt 0.06g

Vodka & cranberry blush

A sophisticated dinner-party cocktail with a crisp cranberry kick.

TAKES 10 MINUTES ● MAKES 12
200ml/7fl oz each vodka and Cointreau
600ml/1 pint cranberry juice
400ml/14fl oz orange juice
crushed ice
pared zest 2–3 limes

1 Pour the vodka and Cointreau into a jug, then add the cranberry and orange juices. Stir well.
2 Fill twelve glasses with the crushed ice, then pour over the cocktail. Finish each glass with a strip of lime peel.

PER COCKTAIL 133 kcals, protein 0.2g, carbs 13g, fat none, sat fat none, fibre none, sugar 7g, salt none

Black olive & goat's cheese tartlets

Stylish veggie bite-sized treats that are perfect for a posh party – make them ahead and they can be chilled until you're ready to bake.

TAKES 40 MINUTES ● MAKES 20

375g pack ready-rolled puff pastry
1 egg, lightly beaten
2 × 200g packs crumbly goat's cheese
handful pitted black olives, sliced
chopped parsley, to garnish

1 Heat oven to 200C/180C fan/gas 6. Unwrap the puff pastry and, using a 5cm cutter, cut out 20 rounds (you may need to re-roll the trimmings to get 20 circles). Now use a slightly smaller cutter to make a light dent in the pastry, creating a rim. Use a fork to make a few pricks in the centre of the pastry; this will stop it from rising, while letting the outer rim puff up.

2 Put the pastry discs on a baking sheet and brush all over with the egg. Crumble the goat's cheese in the centre of each tartlet and scatter over the olives. They can be made to this point up to 2 days ahead and kept in the fridge.

3 Cook for 15–18 minutes until the pastry is puffed and golden brown. Sprinkle with parsley before serving.

PER TARTLET 117 kcals, protein 4g, carbs 7g, fat 8g, sat fat 4g, fibre none, sugar none, salt 0.42g

Teriyaki beef & lettuce cups

Add a taste of Asia to your next party with these irresistible, easy-to-pick-up finger food favourites.

TAKES 25 MINUTES ● MAKES 6

350g/12oz trimmed sirloin steak
2 tbsp teriyaki marinade
½ cucumber
2 tbsp roughly chopped coriander
juice ½ lime
6 Little Gem lettuce leaves
1 red chilli, deseeded and thinly sliced
½ red onion, thinly sliced

1 Put the steak between two sheets of cling film and beat with a rolling pin until half its original thickness. Thinly slice the steak, then mix with the teriyaki marinade in a bowl. Leave to marinate for 5–10 minutes.

2 Roughly dice the cucumber and mix with the chopped coriander and lime juice. Season with a little salt.

3 Heat a frying pan until very hot, then fry the steak slices for 1½–2½ minutes for rare to medium, turning the slices halfway through.

4 Pile the cucumber mixture into the six lettuce leaves, then top with the seared teriyaki beef, chilli and red onion.

PER SERVING 424 kcals, protein 27g, carbs 4g, fat 33g, sat fat 9g, fibre 4g, sugar 4g, salt 0.19g

Pea & feta toasts

This spin on bruschetta tops baguette slices with crushed peas, mint and salty cheese – great for canapés.

TAKES 15 MINUTES ● MAKES 15

300g/10oz frozen peas, left at room
    temperature to defrost
3 tbsp low-fat natural yogurt
2 tbsp chopped mint, plus a few extra
    leaves, torn
zest and juice ½ lemon
15 slices cut from a thin baguette,
    lightly toasted
85g/3oz feta, crumbled
drizzle olive oil

1 Put the defrosted peas, yogurt, chopped mint, lemon zest and juice and some seasoning in a bowl. Roughly mash with a potato masher.

2 Divide the pea mixture among the toasts, then scatter a little feta on top of each with some more black pepper. Arrange on a plate, scatter with more mint leaves and a drizzle of oil. Serve.

PER TOAST: 204 kcals, protein 10g, carbs 27.3g, fat 5.7g, sat fat 2.8g, fibre 4.4g, sugar 6g, salt 1g

Sweet potato & ginger parcels

These moreish snacks are made with Tunisian brik pastry. Similar to filo, but crispier, it's well worth keeping a pack in the freezer, but filo will also work well in this recipe.

TAKES 1¼ HOURS ● MAKES 15

400g/14oz sweet potatoes
50g/2oz melted butter, plus a knob extra
1 red chilli, deseeded and finely chopped
4 spring onions, finely sliced
thumb-sized piece ginger, grated
½ × 190g pack feuilles de brik pastry or 5 sheets filo pastry
few pinches ground cinnamon, to dust

1 Microwave or oven-cook the potatoes until tender. Melt a knob of butter in a pan. Fry the chilli for 30 seconds, then the spring onion whites and ginger for 1 minute. Scrape the flesh from the potatoes, discard the skins, then mash into the pan. Season, then stir in the onion greens.

2 Heat oven to 200C/180C fan/gas 6. Unroll a pastry sheet and cut three 6cm/2¼in strips from the middle; discard leftovers. Brush the strips with melted butter, put a spoonful of potato mix at one end, then fold up from side-to-side to make a triangular parcel. The filling should be completely sealed in. Arrange the parcels on a baking sheet, brush with butter and repeat until you've used up all the filling.

3 Bake for 20 minutes until crisp and golden. Dust with a pinch of cinnamon; then serve.

PER PARCEL 65 kcals, protein 1g, carbs 9g, fat 3g, sat fat 2g, fibre 1g, sugar 2g, salt 0.27g

Tia Maria cheesecake

Perfect for New Year's Eve or any other festive celebration, this American-style dessert really has the wow-factor.

TAKES 1 HOUR, PLUS OVERNIGHT CHILLING • SERVES 16

FOR THE BISCUIT CRUST

85g/3½oz hot melted butter, plus extra butter for greasing

14 plain chocolate digestives, finely crushed

FOR THE CHEESECAKE

3 × 300g packs full-fat soft cheese, at room temperature

200g/7oz golden caster sugar

4 tbsp plain flour

2 tsp vanilla extract

2 tbsp Tia Maria liqueur

3 eggs

300ml pot soured cream

FOR THE TOPPING

150ml pot soured cream

2 tbsp Tia Maria liqueur

cocoa powder, for dusting

8 Ferrero Rocher chocolates, unwrapped

1 Heat oven to 180C/160C fan/gas 4. Grease and line the base of a 25cm-round springform tin with baking paper. Mix the butter and biscuit crumbs. Press on to the base of the tin, bake for 10 minutes. Cool.

2 Increase the oven temperature to 240C/220C fan/gas 9. Beat the cheese and sugar with a whisk until smooth; whisk in the flour, vanilla, Tia Maria, eggs and the soured cream.

3 Grease the sides of the cake tin with butter. Pour in the mixture. Bake for 10 minutes, then turn the oven down to 110C/90C fan/gas ¼ for 25 minutes. Turn off the oven, then open the door and leave to cool inside the oven for 2 hours. Don't worry if it cracks a little.

4 Meanwhile, make the topping. Mix the soured cream and Tia Maria, then smooth on top of the cheesecake. Chill.

5 To serve, remove from the tin and slide on to a plate. Dust with cocoa. Lightly mark the cheesecake into 16 portions, put a chocolate on every other portion.

PER SERVING 410 kcals, protein 7g, carbs 32g, fat 29g, sat fat 17g, fibre 1g, sugar 24g, salt 0.89g

Bitter chocolate truffles

These truffles make the perfect end to any dinner party. For a lighter, sweeter taste, use a dark chocolate with less cocoa solids.

TAKES 2 HOURS ● MAKES 24

2 × 100g bars dark chocolate, 70%
   cocoa solids, chopped
85ml/3fl oz double cream
1 tsp vanilla extract
cocoa powder or grated white
   chocolate, for dusting

1 Put the dark chocolate, cream and vanilla in a pan and heat very gently until melted. Transfer to a bowl, cool, then chill for 1½ hours until firm.

2 Use a mini ice-cream scoop or teaspoon to make 24 truffles, then dust them with cocoa or grated white chocolate. Chill until ready to eat. You can make these 4 days ahead or they will freeze for 1 month. To serve, thaw in a cool place and, if needed, dust with a little more cocoa or chocolate.

PER TRUFFLE 62 kcals, protein 1g, carbs 5g, fat 4g, sat fat 3g, fibre none, sugar 5g, salt none

Crispy neeps 'n' tatties cake

If you're having friends round for Burns Night, this Scottish twist on a rösti goes well with game, duck breast or roast chicken as well as the more traditional haggis.

TAKES 1 HOUR 20 MINUTES
- **SERVES 6**

1 large swede, peeled and cut into chunks
4 baking potatoes, peeled and cut into chunks
50g/2oz butter
sunflower oil, for greasing
8 thin slices pancetta

1 Boil the swede and potatoes in salted water for about 20 minutes until completely tender, then drain well. Return to the pan on a very low heat for a few minutes to dry out. Off the heat, bash the veg into a chunky mash with half the butter, a touch of salt and lots of pepper.
2 Heat oven to 220C/200C fan/gas 7. Grease an ovenproof frying pan or loose-bottomed tart tin with a splash of oil and line the pan with the pancetta so it meets in the middle (like the stripes on the Union flag). Press the veg into the dish, dot with the remaining butter, then bake for about 40 minutes until crisp and golden. Remove from the oven, turn out on to a board and cut into wedges.

PER SERVING 267 kcals, protein 6g, carbs 31g, fat 14g, sat fat 6g, fibre 5g, sugar 8g, salt 0.75g

Cranachan

A true taste of Scotland and the perfect end to a Burns Night dinner party.

TAKES 20 MINUTES • SERVES 4
2 tbsp medium oatmeal
300g/10oz fresh British raspberries
a little caster sugar
350ml/12fl oz double cream
2 tbsp clear heather honey
2–3 tbsp whisky, to taste

1 To toast the oatmeal, spread it out on a baking sheet and grill it until it smells rich and nutty. It will darken quickly, so check it often and use your sense of smell to tell you when it is nutty enough. Let cool.

2 Make a raspberry purée by crushing half the fruit and sieving it into a bowl. Sweeten to taste with a little caster sugar.

3 Whisk the double cream until just set, and stir in the honey and whisky, trying not to over-whip the cream. Taste the mix and add a little more of either if need be. Stir in the oatmeal and whisk lightly until the mixture is just firm.

4 Alternate layers of the cream with the remaining whole raspberries and purée in four serving dishes. Allow to chill slightly before eating.

PER SERVING 529 kcals, protein 3g, carbs 18g, fat 48g, sat fat 27g, fibre 2g, sugar 13g, salt 0.06g

Tiramisu with honeycomb crunch

Adding a little homemade honeycomb to this tiramisu finishes it off beautifully, and your Valentine is guaranteed to be impressed!

TAKES 40 MINUTES, PLUS CHILLING
- **SERVES 2**

1 egg yolk
2 tbsp caster sugar
¼ tsp vanilla paste or extract
85g/3oz mascarpone
150ml/¼ pint double cream
2 tbsp Kahlúa coffee liqueur
5 tbsp very strong coffee
85g/3oz sponge fingers
cocoa powder, for dusting

FOR THE HONEYCOMB

a little mild oil, such as sunflower, for greasing
85g/3oz caster sugar
2 tbsp clear honey
1 tsp bicarbonate of soda

1 Whisk the egg yolk with the caster sugar and vanilla until pale. Add the mascarpone and cream, then beat with an electric whisk until smooth and thick.

2 Put the Kahlúa and coffee in a bowl and dip in enough sponge fingers to cover the bottoms of two small bowls or ramekins. Cover with half the creamy mixture, repeat with some more soaked biscuits, topping with more creamy mixture, until your dishes are full. Dust with a little cocoa powder and chill for at least 2 hours or overnight.

3 For the honeycomb, oil a baking sheet or tin or line with a non-stick mat. Gently heat the sugar and honey with a splash of water in a heavy-based pan until melted. Increase the heat and bubble to a good caramel colour, then lift off the heat, whisk in the bicarb and tip on to the baking sheet or tin to cool. Once cold, crush with a rolling pin or thinly slice into shards, and scatter a little over the tiramisus to serve.

PER SERVING 973 kcals, protein 8g, carbs 87g, fat 66g, sat fat 37g, fibre 1g, sugar 73g, salt 1g

Baileys & chocolate creams

Just a few spoonfuls of this rich and creamy dessert are all you need to end your Valentine's meal with a flourish.

TAKES 25 MINUTES, PLUS CHILLING
● **MAKES 2**

50g/2oz dark chocolate, 70% cocoa
  solids, broken into squares
150ml/¼ pint double cream
2 tbsp Baileys
cocoa powder, for dusting
biscotti or amaretti biscuits,
  to serve

1 Put the chocolate into a bowl. Mix the cream with the Baileys, reserve 2 tablespoons, then tip the rest into a pan and bring just to the boil. Remove from the heat and tip straight over the chocolate, stirring until the chocolate melts. Divide between two small glasses and allow to cool slightly.

2 Whip the remaining Baileys cream until slightly thickened, then spoon over the cooled chocolate mix. Chill for at least 1 hour to set. While you're waiting, cut out a heart shape from a piece of thick card.

3 When ready to serve, set the card over the glass and sift over a dusting of cocoa powder. Lift off carefully and do the same with the other glass. Serve with biscotti or amaretti biscuits on the side.

PER GLASS 566 kcals, protein 3g, carbs 17g, fat 51g, sat fat 28g, fibre 2g, sugar 12g, salt 0.05g

Black velvet baby cakes

These gorgeous Guinness puds are an indulgent treat – and perfect for any St Patrick's Day dinner party.

TAKES 1 HOUR • MAKES 6

100g/4oz softened butter, plus extra
    for greasing
175g/6oz light brown soft sugar
1 egg
100g/4oz self-raising flour
50g/2oz ground almonds
½ tsp bicarbonate of soda
5 tbsp cocoa powder, plus a little extra
    for decorating
150ml/¼ pint Guinness

FOR THE CREAM

200ml/7fl oz double cream
25g/1oz icing sugar
splash champagne (optional)

1 Heat oven to 180C/160C fan/gas 4. Grease and line the bases of six dariole moulds with baking parchment. Put the butter, sugar, egg, flour, ground almonds, bicarbonate, cocoa and Guinness in a mixing bowl. Beat together until lump-free. Divide among the tins then bake for 20–25 minutes until risen and a skewer poked in comes out clean. Cool for 15 minutes, then remove them from the tins and let them cool completely on a wire rack the same way up they were baked – don't turn them upside-down.

2 Whip the cream with the icing sugar and splash of champagne, if using, until thick. Spoon a dollop on to the top of each cake and dust with cocoa. Serve with glasses of champagne or Black Velvet cocktails.

PER CAKE 587 kcals, protein 5g, carbs 52g, fat 41g, sat fat 21g, fibre 2g, sugar 36g, salt 0.59g

Hooting Halloween owls

Delicious and simple chocolate cupcakes that will please everyone at your Halloween party – not just the kids.

TAKES 1½ HOURS • MAKES 12

300g/10oz butter, softened
300g/10oz golden caster sugar
200g self-raising flour
1 rounded tbsp cocoa powder
6 medium eggs

FOR ICING & DECORATION

200g/7oz butter, softened
280g icing sugar, sifted
1 tube orange ready-to-use icing
1 small bag Maltesers
1 small bag mini chocolate buttons
1 tub jelly diamonds (just the orange ones)

1 Heat oven to 190C/170C fan/gas 5. Line a 12-cup muffin tin with brown muffin cases. Beat the cake ingredients to a smooth batter and divide among the cases, almost filling them to the top. You may have a little left over. Bake for 20–25 minutes until risen and spongy. Cool on a wire rack.

2 To decorate, beat the butter and icing sugar for the icing until smooth. Slice off the very tops of the cakes and cut each piece in half. Spread a generous layer of icing over each cake.

3 Working on one cake at a time, squirt a pea-sized blob of orange icing on to two Maltesers and use to fix a chocolate button on each. Sit the eyes, two pieces of cake top (curved edge up) and a jelly diamond on the icing to make an owl.

PER CAKE 615 kcals, protein 6g, carbs 68g, fat 38g, sat fat 23g, fibre 1g, sugar 54g, salt 1g

Little frosty Christmas cakes

These delightful mini fruitcakes make a perfect dessert or a gift for friends to take home after a Christmas party.

TAKES 1½ HOURS • MAKES 8

200g/7oz butter, softened, plus extra
    for greasing
200g/7oz dark muscovado sugar
3 eggs, beaten
1 tbsp black treacle
200g/7oz self-raising flour
2 tsp mixed spice
1 tsp baking powder
2 eating apples (about 100g/4oz each),
    grated
300g/10oz mixed sultanas and dates

FOR THE DECORATION
2 tbsp apricot jam
500g/1lb 2oz natural marzipan
500g/1lb 2oz ready-to-roll white icing
1 egg white
50g/2oz caster sugar
16 fresh cranberries
1 bunch rosemary
50g/2oz icing sugar

1 Heat oven to 180C/160C fan/gas 4. Butter eight 150ml ramekins and line with baking paper. Beat the cake ingredients (except fruit) together. Fold in the fruit.

2 Put the cake mix in the ramekins. Bake for 30 minutes. Allow to cool slightly and turn out on to a wire rack.

3 Heat the jam with 1 tablespoon of water; brush over the cakes. Lightly knead the marzipan; shape into eight balls. Roll these into flat circles, about 1cm/½in diameter, the same size as the cakes. Stick the marzipan to the jammy side of the cakes, then do the same with the icing, brushing the marzipan with a little cooled boiled water to help it stick.

4 Beat the egg white until frothy. Spread the caster sugar on a plate. Dip the cranberries and rosemary in the egg white and roll in the caster sugar. Leave to dry. Tip away all but 2 teaspoons of the egg white; mix with the icing sugar to form a paste. Use this to fix a sprig of rosemary and two cranberries to each cake.

PER CAKE 1084 kcals, protein 14g, carbs 168g, fat 39g, sat fat 15g, fibre 3g, sugar 151g, salt 1g

Christmas pudding cake pops

These lollipops are a fantastic festive treat for kids and make an impressive centrepiece too.

TAKES 2 HOURS ● MAKES 10

150g/5oz bar white chocolate
1 orange, zest finely grated
200g/7oz shop-bought Madeira cake, pulsed to crumbs in food processor

TO ICE & DECORATE

300g/10oz dark chocolate, 60–70% cocoa solids, broken into chunks
50g/2oz white chocolate, broken into chunks
sugar holly decorations or red and green writing icing

1 Melt the white chocolate in a bowl over just simmering water or in the microwave. Stir in the orange zest; work this mix into the cake crumbs.

2 Form into ten truffle-sized balls. Arrange on a baking parchment-lined plate and chill for 30 minutes.

3 Melt the dark chocolate. Dip a lolly stick into the melted chocolate; poke halfway into a cake ball. Repeat with the other balls. Put them back on the plate; return to the fridge for 5 minutes.

4 Dip the cake pops one at a time into the melted chocolate, spinning them to even out the surface. Stand the pops into a piece of polystyrene, keeping them apart. Allow to set for about half an hour.

4 Melt the white chocolate. Allow to cool to a thick, runny consistency. Spoon a small amount on top of the cake pops. Pop one holly decoration on the top. If using writing icing, wait 20 minutes until the white chocolate has set. Pipe on holly leaves and two red dots for berries.

PER CAKE POP: 334 kcals, protein 4g, carbs 40g, fat 18g, sat fat 10g, fibre 1g, sugar 36g, salt 0.3g

Mimosas

Kick off your Christmas Day with this simple classic cocktail, which works with any sparkling wine, champagne or prosecco.

TAKES 10 MINUTES ● MAKES 6

1 bottle champagne or sparkling wine, chilled
1 litre/1¾ pints freshly squeezed orange juice, chilled

1 Half-fill each of six glasses with champagne, then carefully pour in the orange juice until the glass is full then serve.

PER COCKTAIL 147 kcals, protein 1g, carbs 20g, fat none, sat fat none, fibre none, sugar 20g, salt 0.02g

Merry cherry fizz

Start your New Year celebrations in style with a glass of pretty fizz – cherry brandy, kirsch, amaretto and vodka, topped up with sparking grape juice.

TAKES 10 MINUTES • MAKES 6

50ml/2fl oz cherry brandy liqueur
50ml/2fl oz kirsch
50ml/2fl oz amaretto
100ml/4fl oz vodka
750ml bottle sparkling red grape juice
   (we used Shloer)
12 maraschino cherries

1 Pour the cherry brandy liqueur, kirsch, amaretto and vodka into a jug or cocktail shaker, and mix well.

2 Divide among six tall glasses and top up with the grape juice. Add two maraschino cherries to each glass and serve.

PER FIZZ 328 kcals, protein none, carbs 19g, fat none, sat fat none, fibre none, sugar 19g, salt none

Index

Also available from BBC Books and *Good Food*